Excerpts From Sister Niveditas Book

by

Swami Vivekananda

Double 9 BOOKS

Excerpts From Sister Niveditas Book

by Swami Vivekananda

ISBN: 978-93-59393-66-7

Published by

DOUBLE 9 BOOKS
2/13-B, Ansari Road
Daryaganj, New Delhi – 110002
info@double9books.com
www.double9books.com
Tel. 011-40042856

ABOUT THE AUTHOR

Swami Vivekananda was born Narendranath Datta in India on January 12, 1863. He died on July 4, 1902, and was the most important student of the Indian saint Ramakrishna. He was an important part of bringing Vedanta and Yoga to the West. He is also charged with making people more aware of other religions and making Hinduism a major world religion. Vivekananda had a lot of success at the Parliament. In the years that followed, he gave hundreds of lectures across the United States, England, and Europe to spread the main ideas of Hinduism. He also started the Vedanta Society of New York and the Vedanta Society of San Francisco, which is now the Vedanta Society of Northern California. Both of these groups became the basis for Vedanta Societies in the West. Vivekananda was one of the most important philosophers and social reformers in India at the time. He was also one of the most successful and powerful Vedanta missionaries in the West.People now think of him as one of the most important people in modern India and Hinduism. Mahatma Gandhi said that after reading Vivekananda's works, he loved his country a thousand times more.

CONTENTS

Notes Of Some Wanderings With The Swami Vivekananda

[Excerpts from the book by Sister Nivedita]

Note: In the following work only those extracts which present Swami Vivekananda's ideas or direct quotations have been printed. Descriptions marking the background context of these talks have also been retained for the sake of clarity and continuity. Ellipses mark the deleted portions. Spelling and punctuation have been made to conform to the style of the *Complete Works*.

Foreword

PERSONS: The Swami Vivekananda, Gurubhais, (Spiritual brethren; disciples of one and the same master are so called.) and a party of European guests and disciples, amongst whom were Dhira Mata, the "Steady Mother" [Mrs. Ole Bull]; one whose name was Jaya [Miss Josephine MacLeod]; and Sister Nivedita. (Dhira Mata and Jaya were Americans; Nivedita was British.)

PLACE: Different parts of India.

TIME: The year 1898.

Beautiful have been the days of this year. In them the Ideal has become the Real. First in our riverside cottage at Belur; then in the Himalayas, at Naini Tal and Almora; afterwards wandering here and there through Kashmir — everywhere have come hours never to be forgotten, words that will echo through our lives forever, and once, at least, a glimpse of the Beatific Vision.

It has been all play.

We have seen a love that would be one with the humblest and most ignorant, seeing the world for the moment through his eyes, as if criticism were not; we have laughed over the colossal caprice of genius; we have warmed ourselves at heroic fires; and we have been present, as it were, at the awakening of the Holy Child.

But there has been nothing grim or serious about any of these things. Pain has come close to all of us. Solemn anniversaries have been and gone. But sorrow was lifted into a golden light, where it was made radiant and did not destroy.

Fain, if I could, would I describe our journeys. Even as I write I see the irises in bloom at Baramulla; the young rice beneath the poplars at Islamabad; starlight scenes in Himalayan forests; and the royal beauties of Delhi and the Taj. One longs to attempt some memorial of these. It would be worse than useless. Not, then, in words, but in the light of memory they are enshrined forever, together with the kindly and gentle folk who dwell among them and whom we trust always to have left the gladder for our coming.

We have learnt something of the mood in which new faiths are born and of the persons who inspire such faiths. For we have been with one who drew all men to him — listening to all, feeling with all and refusing none. We have known a humility that wiped out all littleness, a renunciation that would die for scorn of oppression and pity of the oppressed, a love that would bless even the oncoming feet of torture and of death. We have joined hands with that woman who washed the feet of the Lord with her tears and wiped them with the hairs of her head. We have lacked not the occasion, but her passionate consciousness of self.

Seated under a tree in the garden of dead emperors there came to us a vision of all the rich and splendid things of Earth, offering themselves as a shrine for the great of soul. The storied windows of cathedrals and the jewelled thrones of kings, the banners of great captains and the vestments of the priests, the pageants of cities and the retreats of the proud — all came and all were rejected.

In the garments of the beggar, despised by the alien, worshipped by the people, we have seen him; and only the bread of toil, the shelter of cottage roofs, and the common road across the cornfields seem real enough for the background to this life.. . . Amongst his own the ignorant loved him as much as scholars and statesmen. The boatmen watched the river, in his absence, for his return, and servants disputed with guests to do him service. And through it all the veil of playfulness was never dropped. "They played with the Lord" and instinctively they knew it.

To those who have known such hours, life is richer and sweeter, and in the long nights even the wind in the palm trees seems to cry: "Mahadeva! Mahadeva! Mahadeva!"

I.
The House On The Ganges

PLACE: A cottage at Belur, beside the Ganges.

TIME: March to May, 1898.

Of the home by the Ganges the Master had said to one, "You will find that little house of Dhira Mata like heaven, for it is all love, from beginning to end.

It was so indeed. Within, an unbroken harmony, and without, everything alike beautiful — the green stretch of grass, the tall cocoanut palms, the little brown villages in the jungle, and the Nilkantha that built her nest in a tree — top beside us, on purpose to bring us the blessings of Shiva. In the morning the shadows lay behind the house, but in the afternoons we could sit in front worshipping the Ganges herself — great leonine mother! — and in sight of Dakshineswar.

There came one and another with traditions of the past, and we learnt of the Master's eight years' wanderings; of the name changed from village to village; of the Nirvikalpa Samâdhi; and of that sacred sorrow, too deep for words or for common sight, that one who loved had alone seen. And there too came the Master himself, with his stories of Umâ and Shiva, of Râdhâ and Krishna, and his fragments of song and poetry.

It seemed as if he knew that the first material of a new consciousness must be a succession of vivid but isolated experiences, poured out without proper sequence so as to provoke the mind of the learner to work for its own conception of order and relation.... For the most part it was the Indian religions that he portrayed for us—today dealing with one and tomorrow with another — his choice guided, seemingly, by the whim of the moment. But it was not religion only that he poured out upon us. Sometimes it would be history. Again, it would be folk-lore. On still another occasion it would be the manifold anomalies and inconsistencies of race, caste and custom. In fact India herself became, as heard in him, as the last and noblest of the Purânas, uttering itself through his lips.

Another point in which he had caught a great psychological secret was that of never trying to soften for us that which would at first sight be difficult or repellent. In matters Indian he would rather put forward, in its extreme form at the beginning of our experience, all that might seem impossible for European minds to enjoy. Thus he would quote, for instance, some verses about Gauri and Shankar in a single form:

> On one side grows the hair in long black curls,
> And on the other, corded like rope.
> On one side are seen the beautiful garlands,
> On the other, bone earrings and snake-like coils.
> One side is white with ashes, like the snow mountains,
> The other, golden as the light of dawn.
> For He, the Lord, took a form,
> And that was a divided form,
> Half-woman and half-man

. . . .

Whatever might be the subject of the conversation, it ended always on the note of the infinite. . . . He might appear to take up any subject — literary, ethnological or scientific — but he always made us feel it as an illustration of the Ultimate Vision. There was for him nothing secular. He had a loathing for bondage and a horror of those who "cover chains with flowers", but he never failed to make the true critic's distinction between this and the highest forms of art.

One day we were receiving European guests and he entered into a long talk about Persian poetry. Then suddenly, finding himself quoting the poem that says, "For one mole on the face of my Beloved, I would give all the wealth of Samarkand!" he turned and said energetically, "I would not give a straw, you know, for the man who was incapable of appreciating a love song!" His talk too teemed with epigrams.

It was that same afternoon, in the course of a long political argument, that he said, "In order to become a nation, it appears that *we need a common hate* as well as a common love".

Several months later he remarked that before one who had a mission he never talked of any of the gods save Uma and Shiva. For Shiva and the Mother made the great workers. Yet I have sometimes wondered if he knew at this time how the end of every theme was Bhakti. Much as he dreaded the luxury of spiritual emotion for those who might be enervated by it, he could not help giving glimpses of what it meant to be consumed with the intoxication of God. And so he would chant for us such poems as:

> They have made Radha queen, in the beautiful groves of
> Vrindaban.

At her gate stands Krishna, on guard.
His flute is singing all the time:
Radha is about to distribute infinite wealth of love.
Though I am guard, all the world may enter.
Come all ye who thirst! Say only 'Glory unto Radha!'
Enter the region of love!

Or he would give us the great antiphonal Chorus of the Cowherds, written by his friend: (The Bengali dramatist Girish Chandra Ghosh.)

Men: Thou art the Soul of souls,

Thou yellow-garbed, With thy blue eyes.

Women: Thou dark One! Thou Shepherd of Vrindaban!
Kneeling at the feet of the Shepherdesses.

Men: My soul sings the praise of the glory of the Lord, Who took the human form.

Women: Thy beauty for us, the Gopis. Men: Thou Lord of Sacrifice.

Saviour of the weak.

Women: Who lovest Radha and thy body floats on its

own tears.

. . . . . .

MARCH 25.

. . . At this time the Swami kept the custom of coming to the cottage early and spending the morning hours there, and again returning in the late afternoon. On the second morning of this visit, however — Friday, the Christian feast of the Annunciation — he took us all three back to the Math, and there in the worship-room was held a little service of initiation where one was made a Brahmachârini. That was the happiest of mornings.

After the service we were taken upstairs. The Swami put on the ashes and bone-earrings and matted locks of a Shiva-Yogi and sang and played to us — Indian music on Indian instruments — for an hour.

And in the evening in our boat on the Ganges, he opened his heart to us and told us much of his questions and anxieties regarding the trust that he held from his own Master.

Another week and he was gone to Darjeeling; and till the day that the plague declaration brought him back, we saw him again no more.

MAY 3.

Then two of us met him in the house of our Holy Mother. The political sky was black. It seemed as if a storm were about to burst. . . . Plague, panic and riot were doing their fell work. And the Master turned to the two and said, "There are some who scoff at the existence of Kâli. Yet today She is out there amongst the people. They are frantic with fear, and the soldiery have been called to deal out death. Who can say that God does not manifest Himself as evil as well as good? But only the Hindu dares to worship Him in the evil".

He had come back and the old life was resumed once more, as far as could be, seeing that an epidemic was in prospect and that measures were on hand to give the people confidence. As long as this possibility darkened the horizon, he would not leave Calcutta. But it passed away, and those happy days with it, and the time came that we should go.

II.
At Naini Tal And Almora

PERSONS: The Swami Vivekananda, Gurubhâis, and a party of Europeans and disciples, amongst whom were Dhira Mata, the "Steady Mother"; one whose name was Jaya; and Nivedita.

PLACE: The Himalayas.

TIME: May 11 to May 25, 1898.

We were a large party, or, indeed, two parties, that left Howrah station on Wednesday evening and on Friday morning came in sight of the Himalayas. . . .

Naini Tal was made beautiful by three things — the Master's pleasure in introducing to us his disciple the Raja of Khetri; the dancing girls who met us and asked us where to find him, and were received by him in spite of the remonstrances of others; and by the Mohammedan gentleman who said, "Swamiji, if in after-times any claim you as an Avatâra, an especial incarnation of the Deity — remember that I, a Mohammedan, am the first!"

It was here too that we heard a long talk on Ram Mohan Roy in which he pointed out three things as the dominant notes of this teacher's message — his acceptance of the Vedanta, his preaching of patriotism, and the love that embraced the Mussulman equally with the Hindu. In all these things he claimed himself to have taken up the task that the breadth and foresight of Ram Mohan Roy had mapped out.

The incident of the dancing girls occurred in consequence of our visit to the two temples at the head of the tarn. . . . Here, offering worship, we found two nautch-women. When they had finished, they came up to us, and we, in broken language, entered into conversation with them. We took them for respectable ladies of the town and were much astonished later at the storm which had evidently passed over the Swami's audience at his refusal to have them turned away. Am I mistaken in thinking that it was in connection with these dancing-women of Naini Tal that he first told us the story, many times repeated, of the nautch-girl of Khetri? He had been angry at the invitation to see her, but being prevailed upon to come, she sang:

O Lord, look not upon my evil qualities!
Thy name, O Lord, is Same-Sightedness.
Make us both the same Brahman!

One piece of iron is the knife in the hand of the butcher,
And another piece of iron is the image in the temple.
But when they touch the philosopher's stone,
Both alike turn to gold!

One drop of water is in the sacred Jamuna,
And one is foul in a ditch by the roadside.
But when they fall into the Ganges,
Both alike become holy!

So, Lord, look not upon my evil qualities!
Thy name, O Lord, is Same-Sightedness.
Make us both the same Brahman!

And then, said the Master of himself, the scales fell from his eyes, and seeing that all are indeed one, he condemned no more. . . .

It was late in the afternoon when we left Naini Tal for Almora, and night overtook us while still travelling through the forest. . . . till we reached a quaintly placed Dak bungalow, on the mountain side in the midst of trees. There after some time Swamiji arrived with his party, full of fun and keen in his appreciation of everything that concerned the comfort of his guests. . . .

From the day that we arrived at Almora the Swami renewed his habit of coming over to us at our early breakfast and spending some hours in talk. Then and always he was an exceedingly light sleeper, and I imagine that his visit to us, early as the hour might be, was often paid during the course of his return with his monks from a still earlier walk. Sometimes, but rarely, we saw him again in the evening, either meeting him when out for a walk or going ourselves to Captain Sevier's, where he and his party were staying, and seeing him there. And once he came at that time to call on us.

Into these morning talks at Almora a strange new element, painful but salutary to remember, had crept. There appeared to be on the one side a curious bitterness and distrust, and on the other, irritation and defiance. The youngest of the Swami's disciples at this time, it must be remembered, was an English woman, and of how much this fact meant intellectually — what a strong bias it implied, and always does imply, in the reading of India, what an idealism of the English race and all their deeds and history — the Swami himself had had no conception till the day after her initiation at the monastery. Then he had asked her some exultant question, as to which nation she now belonged, and had been startled to find with what a passion of loyalty and worship she regarded the English flag, giving to it much of the feeling that an Indian woman would give to her Thakur. His surprise and disappointment at the moment were scarcely perceptible. A startled look, no more. Nor did his discovery of the superficial way in which this disciple had joined herself with his people in any degree affect his confidence and courtesy during the remaining weeks spent in the plains.

But with Almora it seemed as if a going-to-school had commenced. . . . It was never more than this; never the dictating of opinion or creed; never more than emancipation from partiality. Even at the end of the terrible experience when this method, as regarded race and country, was renounced, never to be taken up systematically again, the Swami did not call for any confession of faith, any declaration of new opinion. He dropped the whole question. His listener went free. But he had revealed a different standpoint in thought and feeling, so completely and so strongly as to make it impossible for her to rest, until later, by her own labours, she had arrived at a view in which both these partial presentments stood rationalized and accounted for.

"Really, patriotism like yours is sin!" he exclaimed once, many weeks later, when the process of obtaining an uncoloured judgement on some incident had been more than commonly exasperating. "All that I want you to see is that most people's actions are the expression of self-interest, and you constantly oppose to this the idea that a certain race are all angels. Ignorance so determined is wickedness!" . . .

These morning talks at Almora, then, took the form of assaults upon deep-rooted preconceptions — social, literary and artistic — or of long comparisons of Indian and European history and sentiments, often containing extended observations of very great value. One characteristic of the Swami was the habit of attacking the abuses of a country or society openly and vigorously when he was in its midst, whereas after he had left it, it would often seem as if nothing but its virtues were remembered by him. He was always testing his disciples, and the manner of these particular discourses was probably adopted in order to put to the proof the courage and sincerity of one who was both woman and European.

III.
Morning Talks At Almora

PLACE: Almora.

TIME: May and June, 1898.

The first morning the talk was that of the central ideals of civilization — in the West, truth; in the East, chastity. He justified Hindu marriage customs as springing from the pursuit of this ideal and from the woman's need of protection, in combination. And he traced out the relation of the whole subject to the philosophy of the Absolute.

Another morning he began by observing that as there were four main castes — Brahmin, Kshatriya, Bâniyâ [Vaishya], Shudra — so there were four great national functions: the religious or priestly, fulfilled by the Hindus; the military, by the Roman Empire; the mercantile, by England today; and the democratic, by America in the future. And here he launched off into a glowing prophetic forecast of how America would yet solve the problems of the Shudra — the problems of freedom and co-operation — and turned to relate to a non-American listener the generosity of the arrangements which that people had attempted to make for their aborigines.

Again it would be an eager *résumé* of the history of India or of the Moguls, whose greatness never wearied him. Every now and then throughout the summer he would break out into descriptions of Delhi and Agra. Once he described the Taj as "a dimness, and again a dimness, and there — a grave!"

Another time he spoke of Shah Jehan, and then, with a burst of enthusiasm: "Ah! *He* was the glory of his line! A feeling for and discrimination of beauty that are unparalleled in history. And an artist himself! I have seen a manuscript illuminated by him which is one of the art treasures of India. What a genius!"

Oftener still, it was Akbar of whom he would tell, almost with tears in his voice and a passion easier to understand, beside that undomed tomb, open to sun and wind — the grave of Secundra at Agra.

But all the more universal forms of human feeling were open to the Master. In one mood he talked of China as if she were the treasure-house of the world, and told us of the thrill with which he saw inscriptions in old Bengali (Kutil?) characters over the doors of Chinese temples.

Few things could be more eloquent of the vagueness of Western ideas regarding Oriental peoples than the fact that one of his listeners alleged untruthfulness as a notorious quality of that race. . . . The Swami would have none of it. Untruthfulness! Social rigidity! What were these, except very, very relative terms? And as to untruthfulness in particular, could commercial life or social life or any other form of co-operation go on for a day if men did not trust men? Untruthfulness as a necessity of etiquette? And how was that different from the Western idea? Is the Englishman always glad and always sorry at the proper place? But there is still a difference of degree? Perhaps — but only of degree!

Or he might wander as far afield as Italy, that "greatest of the countries of Europe — land of religion and of art; alike of imperial organization and of Mazzini; mother of ideas, of culture and of freedom!

One day it was Shivaji and the Mahrattas and the year's wandering as a Sannyâsin that won him home to Raigarh. "And to this day", said the Swami, "authority in India dreads the Sannyasin, lest he conceals beneath his yellow garb another Shivaji".

Often the enquiry "Who and what are the Aryans?" absorbed his attention; and holding that their origin was complex, he would tell us how in Switzerland he had felt himself to be in China, so like were the types. He believed too that the same was true of some parts of Norway. Then there were scraps of information about countries and physiognomies, an impassioned tale of the Hungarian scholar who traced the Huns to Tibet, and lies buried in Darjeeling and so on. . . .

Sometimes the Swami would deal with the rift between Brahmins and Kshatriyas, painting the whole history of India as a struggle between the two and showing that the latter had always embodied the rising, fetter-destroying impulses of the nation. He could give excellent reason too for the faith that was in him that the Kâyasthas of modern Bengal represented the pre-Mauryan Kshatriyas. He would portray the two opposing types of culture: the one, classical, intensive and saturated with an ever-deepening sense of tradition and custom; the other, defiant, impulsive and liberal in its outlook. It was part of a deep-lying law of the historic development that Râma, Krishna and Buddha had all arisen in the kingly, and not in the priestly caste. And in this paradoxical moment Buddhism was reduced to a caste-smashing formula — "a religion invented by the Kshatriyas" as a crushing rejoinder to Brahminism!

That was a great hour indeed when he spoke of Buddha; for, catching a word that seemed to identify him with its anti—Brahminical spirit, an uncomprehending listener said, "Why, Swami, I did not know that you were a Buddhist!

"Madam", he said, rounding on her, his whole face aglow with the inspiration of that name, "I am the servant of the servants of the servants of Buddha. Who was there ever like him? — the Lord — who never performed one action for himself — with a heart that embraced the whole world! So full of pity that he — prince and monk — would give his life to save a little goat! So loving that he sacrificed himself to the hunger of a tigress! — to the hospitality of a pariah and blessed him! And he came into my room when I was a boy and I fell at his feet! For I knew it was the Lord Himself!

Many times he spoke of Buddha in this fashion, sometimes at Belur and sometimes afterwards. And once he told us the story of Ambâpâli, the beautiful courtesan who feasted him. . . .

National feeling did not have it all its own way. For one morning when the chasm seemed to be widest, there was a long talk on Bhakti — that perfect identity with the Beloved that the devotion of Ray Ramananda, the Bengali nobleman, before Chaitanya so beautifully illustrates:

> Four eyes met. There were changes in two souls.
> And now I cannot remember whether he is a man
> And I a woman, or he a woman and I a man!
> All I know is, there were two, Love came, and
>
> there is one!

It was that same morning that he talked of the Babists of Persia, in their era of martyrdom — of the woman who inspired and the man who worshipped and worked. And doubtless then he expatiated on that theory of his — somewhat quaint and surprising to unaccustomed minds, not so much for the matter of the statement as for the explicitness of the expression — of the greatness and goodness of the young, who can love without seeking personal expression for their love, and their high potentiality.

Another day coming at sunrise when the snows could be seen, dawn-lighted, from the garden, it was Shiva and Umâ on whom he dwelt — and that was Shiva up there, the white snow-peaks, and the light that fell upon Him was the Mother of the World! For a thought on which at this time he was dwelling much was that God is the Universe — not within it or outside it and not the universe God or the image of God, but He it, and the All.

Sometimes all through the summer he would sit for hours telling us stories, those cradle-tales of Hinduism whose function is not at all that of our nursery fictions, but much more like the man-making myths of the old Hellenic world. Best of all these I thought was the story of Shuka, and we looked on the Shiva-mountains and the bleak scenery of Almora the evening we heard it for the first time. . . .

Shuka was indeed the Swami's saint. He was the type, to him, of that highest realization to which life and the world are merely play. Long after, we learned how Shri Ramakrishna had spoken of him in his boyhood as "my Shuka". And never can I forget the look, as of one gazing far into depths of joy, with which he once stood and quoted the words of Shiva in praise of the deep spiritual significance of the Bhagavad-Gitâ and of the greatness of Shuka: "I know the real meaning of the teachings of the Bhagavad-Gita, and Shuka knows, and *perhaps* Vyâsa knows — a little!"

Another day in Almora the Swami talked of the great humanizing lives that had arisen in Bengal, at the long inrolling wash of the first wave of modern consciousness on the ancient shores of Hindu culture. Of Ram Mohan Roy we had already heard from him at Naini Tal. And now of the Pundit Vidyâsâgar he exclaimed, "There is not a man of my age in northern India on whom his shadow has not fallen!" It was a great joy to him to remember that these men and Shri Ramakrishna had all been born within a few miles of each other.

The Swami introduced Vidyasagar to us now as "the hero of widow remarriage and of the abolition of polygamy". But his favourite story about him was of that day when he went home from the Legislative Council, pondering over the question of whether or not to adopt English dress on such occasions. Suddenly someone came up to a fat Mogul who was proceeding homewards in leisurely and pompous fashion in front of him, with the news "Sir, your house is on fire!" The Mogul went neither faster nor slower for this information, and presently the messenger contrived to express a discreet astonishment, whereupon his master turned on him angrily. "Wretch!" he said. "Am I to abandon the gait of my ancestors because a few sticks happen to be burning?" And Vidyasagar, walking behind, determined to stick to the Châdar, Dhoti and sandals, not even adopting coat and slippers.

The picture of Vidyasagar going into retreat for a month for the study of the Shâstras, when his mother had suggested to him the remarriage of child-widows, was very forcible. "He came out of his retirement of opinion that they were *not* against such remarriage, and he obtained the signatures of the pundits that they agreed in this opinion. Then the action of certain native princes led the pundits to abandon their own signatures so that, had the government not determined to assist the movement, it could not have been

carried — and now", added the Swami, "the difficulty has an economic rather than a social basis".

We could believe that a man who was able to discredit polygamy by moral force alone, was "intensely spiritual". And it was wonderful indeed to realize the Indian indifference to a formal creed when we heard how this giant was driven by the famine of 1864 — when 140,000 people died of hunger and disease — to have nothing more to do with God and become entirely agnostic in thought.

With this man, as one of the educators of Bengal, the Swami coupled the name of David Hare, the old Scotsman and atheist to whom the clergy of Calcutta refused Christian burial. He had died of nursing an old pupil through cholera. So his own boys carried his dead body and buried it in a swamp and made the grave a place of pilgrimage. That place has now become College Square, the educational centre, and his school is now within the university. And to this day Calcutta students make pilgrimage to the tomb.

On this day we took advantage of the natural turn of the conversation to cross-question the Swami as to the possible influence that Christianity might have exerted over himself. He was much amused to hear that such a statement had been hazarded, and told us with much pride of his only contact with missionary influences, in the person of his old Scotch master, Mr. Hastie. This hot-headed old man lived on nothing and regarded his room as his boys' home as much as his own. It was he who had first sent the Swami to Shri Ramakrishna, and towards the end of his stay in India he used to say, "Yes, my boy, you were right, you were right! — It is true that all is God!" "I am *proud* of him!" cried the Swami. "But I don't think you could say that he had Christianized me much!" . . .

We heard charming stories too on less serious subjects. There was the lodging-house in an American city, for instance, where he had had to cook his own food, and where he would meet in the course of operations "an actress who ate roast turkey every day, and a husband and wife who lived by making ghosts". And when the Swami remonstrated with the husband and tried to persuade him to give up deceiving people, saying, "You *ought* not to do this!" the wife would come up behind and say eagerly, "Yes, sir! That's just what I tell him; for he makes all the ghosts, and Mrs. Williams takes all the money!"

He told us also of a young engineer, an educated man, who, at a spiritualistic gathering, "when the fat Mrs. Williams appeared from behind the screen as his thin mother, exclaimed, 'Mother dear, how you *have* grown in the spirit-world!' "

"At this", said the Swami, "my heart broke, for I thought there could be no hope for the man". But never at a loss, he told the story of a Russian painter who was ordered to paint the picture of a peasant's dead father, the only description given being, "Man! Don't I tell you he had a wart on his nose?" When at last, therefore, the painter had made a portrait of some stray peasant and affixed a large wart to the nose, the picture was declared to be ready, and the son was told to come and see it. He stood in front of it, greatly overcome, and said, "Father! Father! How changed you are since I saw you last!" After this, the young engineer would never speak to the Swami again, which showed at least that he could see the point of a story. But at this the Hindu monk was genuinely astonished.

In spite of such general interests, however, the inner strife grew high, and the thought pressed on the mind of one of the older members of our party that the Master himself needed service and peace. Many times he spoke with wonder of the torture of life, and who can say how many signs there were of bitter need? A word or two was spoken — little, but enough — and he, after many hours, came back and told us that he longed for quiet and would go alone to the forests and find soothing.

And then, looking up, he saw the young moon shining above us, and he said, "The Mohammedans think much of the new moon. Let us also, with the new moon, begin a new life!" And he blessed his daughter with a great blessing so that she, thinking that her old relationship was broken, nor dreaming that a new and deeper life was being given to it, knew only that the hour was strange and passing sweet. . . .

MAY 25

He went. It was Wednesday. And on Saturday he came back. He had been in the silence of the forests ten hours each day, but on returning to his tent in the evenings he had been surrounded with so much eager attendance as to break the mood, and he had fled. Yet he was radiant. He had discovered in himself the old-time Sannyasin, able to go barefoot and endure heat, cold and scanty fare, unspoilt by the West. . . .

JUNE 2.

. . . . . .

And then, as we sat working on Friday morning the telegram came, a day late, that said: "Goodwin died last night at Ootacamund". Our poor friend had, it appeared, been one of the first victims of what was to prove an epidemic of typhoid fever. And it seemed that with his last breath he had spoken of the Swami and longed for his presence by his side.

JUNE 5.

On Sunday evening the Swami came home. Through our gate and over the terrace his way brought him, and there we sat and talked with him a moment. He did not know our news, but a great darkness hung over him already, and presently he broke the silence to remind us of that saint who had called the cobra's bite "messenger from the Beloved", one whom he had loved second only to Shri Ramakrishna himself. "I have just", he said, "received a letter that says: 'Pavhari Baba has completed all his sacrifices with the sacrifice of his own body. He has burnt himself in his sacrificial fire'". "Swami!" exclaimed someone from amongst his listeners. "Wasn't that very wrong?"

"How can I tell?" said the Swami, speaking in great agitation. "He was too great a man for me to judge. He knew himself what he was doing."

Very little was said after this, and the party of monks passed on. Not yet had the other news been broken.

JUNE 6.

Next morning he came early in a great mood. He had been up, he said afterwards, since four. And one went out to meet him and told him of Mr. Goodwin's death. The blow fell quietly. Some days later he refused to stay in the place where he had received it, and complained of the weakness that brought the image of his most faithful disciple constantly into his mind. It was no more manly, he protested, to be thus ridden by one's memory than to retain the characteristics of the fish or the dog. Man must conquer this illusion and know that the dead are here beside us and with us as much as ever. It is their absence and separation that are a myth. And then he would break out again with some bitter utterance against the folly of imagining Personal Will to guide the universe. "As if", he exclaimed, "it would not be one's right and duty to fight such a God and slay Him for killing Goodwin! And Goodwin, if he had lived, could have done so much!" And in India one was free to recognize this as the most religious, because the most unflinchingly truthful, mood of all!

And while I speak of this utterance, I may perhaps put beside it another that I heard a year later, spoken out of the same fierce wonder at the dreams with which we comfort ourselves. "Why!" he said then. "Every petty magistrate and officer is allowed his period of retirement and rest. Only God, the Eternal Magistrate, must sit judging forever and never go free!"

But in these first hours the Swami was calm about his loss, and sat down and chatted quietly with us. He was full that morning of Bhakti passing into asceticism, the divine passion that carries the soul on its high tides far out of reach of persons, yet leaves it again struggling to avoid those sweet snares of personality.

What he said that morning of renunciation proved a hard gospel to one of those who listened, and when he came again she put it to him as her conviction that to love without attachment involved no pain, and was in itself ideal.

He turned on her with a sudden solemnity. "What is this idea of Bhakti without renunciation?" he said. "It is most pernicious!" And standing there for an hour or more, he talked of the awful self-discipline that one must impose on oneself if one would indeed be unattached, of the requisite nakedness of selfish motives, and of the danger that at any moment the most flower-like soul might have its petals soiled with the grosser stains of life. He told the story of an Indian nun who was asked when a man could be certain of safety on this road, and who sent back for answer a little plate of ashes. For the fight against passion was long and fierce, and at any moment the conqueror might become the conquered. . . .

. . . Weeks afterwards in Kashmir, when he was again talking in some kindred fashion, one of us ventured to ask him if the feeling he thus roused were not that worship of pain that Europe abhors as morbid.

"Is the worship of pleasure, then, so noble?" was his immediate answer. "But indeed", he added after a pause, "we worship neither pain nor pleasure. We seek through either to come at that which transcends them both".

JUNE 9.

This Thursday morning there was a talk on Krishna. It was characteristic of the Swami's mind, and characteristic also of the Hindu culture from which he had sprung, that he could lend himself to the enjoyment and portrayal of an idea one day that the next would see submitted to a pitiless analysis and left slain upon the field. He was a sharer to the full in the belief of his people that, provided an idea was spiritually true and consistent, it mattered very little about its objective actuality. And this mode of thought had first been suggested to him in his boyhood by his own master. He had mentioned some doubt as to the authenticity of a certain religious history. "What!" said Shri Ramakrishna. "Do you not then think that those who could conceive such ideas must have been the thing itself?"

The existence of Krishna, then, like that of Christ, he often told us "in the general way" he doubted. Buddha and Mohammed alone amongst religious teachers had been fortunate enough to have "enemies as well as friends", so that their historical careers were beyond dispute. As for Krishna, he was the most shadowy of all. A poet, a cowherd, a great ruler, a warrior and a sage had all perhaps been merged in one beautiful figure holding the Gitâ in his hand.

But today Krishna was "the most perfect of the Avatâras". And a wonderful picture followed of the charioteer who reined in his horses while he surveyed the field of battle and in one brief glance noted the disposition of the forces, at the same moment that he commenced to utter to his royal pupil the deep spiritual truths of the Gita.

And indeed as we went through the countrysides of northern India this summer, we had many chances of noting how deep this Krishna myth had set its mark upon the people. The songs that dancers chanted as they danced in the roadside hamlets were all of Râdhâ and Krishna. And the Swami was fond of a statement, as to which we, of course, could have no opinion, that the Krishna-worshippers of India had exhausted the possibilities of the romantic motive in lyric poetry. . . .

But throughout these days the Swami was fretting to be away and alone. The place where he had heard of Mr. Goodwin's loss was intolerable to him, and letters to be written and received constantly renewed the wound. He said one day that Shri Ramakrishna, while seeming to be all Bhakti, was really within all Jnana; but he himself, apparently all Jnana, was full of Bhakti, and that thereby he was apt to be as weak as any woman.

One day he carried off a few faulty lines of someone's writing and brought back a little poem, which was sent to the widowed mother as his memorial of her son. . . . [*Vide* "Requiescat in Pace", *Complete Works*, IV]

And then, because there was nothing left of the original and he feared that she who was corrected (because *her* lines had been "in three metres") might be hurt, he expatiated, long and earnestly upon the theme, that it was so much greater to feel poetically than merely to string syllables together in rhyme and metre. He might be very severe on a sympathy or an opinion that seemed in his eyes sentimental or false. But an effort that failed found always in the Master its warmest advocate and tenderest defence.

And how happy was that acknowledgment of the bereaved mother to him when in the midst of her sorrow she wrote and thanked him for the character of his influence over the son who had died so far away!

JUNE 10.

It was our last afternoon at Almora that we heard the story of the fatal illness of Shri Ramakrishna. Dr. Mahendra Lal Sarkar had been called in and had pronounced the disease to be cancer of the throat, leaving the young disciples with many warnings as to its infectious nature. Half an hour later "Naren", as he then was, came in and found them huddled together discussing the dangers of the case. He listened to what they had been told and then, looking down, saw at his feet the cup of gruel that had been partly taken by Shri Ramakrishna and which must have contained in it the germs of the fatal discharges of mucus and pus, as it came out in his baffled attempts to swallow the thing on account of the stricture of the food-passage in the throat. He picked it up and drank from it before them all. Never was the infection of cancer mentioned amongst the disciples again.

IV.
On The Way To Kathgodam

JUNE 11.

On Saturday morning we left Almora. It took us two days and a half to reach Kathgodam. . . .

Somewhere en route near a curious old water-mill and deserted forge, the Swami told Dhira Mata of a legend that spoke of this hill-side as haunted by a race of centaur-like phantoms, and of an experience known to him by which one had first seen forms there and only afterwards heard the folk tale.

The roses were gone by this time, but a flower was in bloom that crumbled at a touch, and he pointed this out because of its wealth of associations in Indian poetry.

JUNE 12.

On Sunday afternoon we rested near the plains in what we took to be an out-of-the-way hotel above a lake and fall, and there he translated for us the Rudra prayer:

> From the unreal lead us to the Real.
> From darkness lead us unto light.
> From death lead us to immortality.
> Reach us through and through our self.
> And evermore protect us — O Thou Terrible! —
> From ignorance, by Thy sweet, compassionate face.

He hesitated a long time over the fourth line, thinking of rendering it, "Embrace us in the heart of our heart". But at last he put his perplexity to us, saying shyly, "The real meaning is, Reach us through and through our self". He had evidently feared that this sentence, with its extraordinary intensity, might not make good sense in English. . . . I have understood that a more literal rendering would be, "O Thou who art manifest only unto Thyself, manifest Thyself also unto us!" I now regard his translation as a rapid and direct transcript of the experience of Samâdhi itself. It tears the living heart out of the Sanskrit, as it were, and renders it again in an English form.

It was indeed an afternoon of translations, and he gave us fragments of the great benediction after mourning, which is one of the most beautiful of the Hindu sacraments:

> The blissful winds are sweet to us.
> The seas are showering bliss on us.
> May the corn in our fields bring bliss to us.
> May the plants and herbs bring bliss to us.
> May the cattle give us bliss.
> O Father in Heaven, be Thou blissful unto us!
> Thy very dust of the earth is full of bliss.

And then, the voice dying down into meditation:

> It is all bliss — all bliss — all bliss.

And again we had Suradâsa's song, which the Swami heard from the nautch-girl at Khetri:

> O Lord, look not upon my evil qualities!
> Thy name, O Lord, is Same-Sightedness.
> Make of us both the same Brahman! . . .

Was it that same day or some other that he told us of the old Sannyâsin in Benares who saw him annoyed by troops of monkeys and, afraid that he might turn and run, shouted, "Always face the brute!"?

Those journeys were delightful. We were always sorry to reach a destination. At this time it took us a whole afternoon to cross the Terai by rail — that strip of malarial country on which, as he reminded us, Buddha had been born.

As we had come down the mountain roads, we had met parties of country-folk fleeing to the upper hills with their families and all their goods, to escape the fever which would be upon them with the rains. And now in the train there was the gradual change of vegetation to watch and the Master's pleasure, greater than that of any proprietor, in showing us the wild peacocks, or here and there an elephant or a train of camels. . . .

V.
On The Way To Baramulla

PERSONS: The Swami Vivekananda, Gurubhais, and a party of Europeans and disciples, amongst whom were Dhira Mata, the "Steady Mother"; one whose name was Jaya; and Nivedita.

PLACE: From Bareilly to Baramulla, Kashmir.

TIME: June 14 to 20, 1898.

JUNE 14.

We entered the Punjab next day, and great was the Swami's excitement at the fact. It almost seemed as if he had been born there, so close and special was his love for this province. He talked of the girls at their spinning wheels listening to the "So'ham! So'ham!" — I am He! I am He! Then, by a swift transition he turned to the far past and unrolled for us the great historic panorama of the advance of the Greeks on the Indus, the rise of Chandragupta and the development of the Buddhistic empire. He was determined this summer to find his way to Attock and see with his own eyes the spot at which Alexander was turned back. He described to us the Gandhara sculptures, which he must have seen in the Lahore Museum the year before, and lost himself in indignant repudiation of the absurd European claim that India had ever sat at the feet of Greece in things artistic.

Then there were flying glimpses of long-expected cities — Ludhiana, where certain trusty English disciples had lived as children; Lahore, where his Indian lectures had ended; and so on. We came too upon the dry gravel beds of many rivers and learnt that the space between one pair was called the Doab and the area containing them all, the Punjab.

It was at twilight, crossing one of these stony tracts, that he told us of that great vision which came to him years ago, while he was still new to the ways of the life of a monk, giving back to him, as he always afterwards believed, the ancient mode of Sanskrit chanting.

"It was evening", he said, "in that age when the Aryans had only reached the Indus. I saw an old man seated on the bank of the great river. Wave upon wave of darkness was rolling in upon him, and he was chanting from the Rig-Veda. Then I awoke and went on chanting. They were the tones that we used long ago".

. . . Those who were constantly preoccupied with imagination regarding their own past always aroused his contempt. But on this occasion of telling the story, he gave a glimpse of it from a very different point of view.

"Shankarâchârya", he was saying, "had caught the rhythm of the Vedas, the national cadence. Indeed I always imagine", he went on suddenly with dreamy voice and far-away look, "I always imagine that he had some vision such as mine when he was young, and recovered the ancient music that way. Anyway, his whole life's work is nothing but that, the throbbing of the beauty of the Vedas and Upanishads". . . .

From Rawalpindi to Murree we went by tonga, and there we spent some days before setting out for Kashmir. Here the Swami came to the conclusion that any effort which he might make to induce the orthodox to accept a European as a fellow-disciple, or in the direction of woman's education, had better be made in Bengal. The distrust of the foreigner was too strong in Punjab to admit of work succeeding there. He was much occupied by this question from time to time, and would sometimes remark on the paradox presented by the Bengali combination of political antagonism to the English, and readiness to love and trust. . . .

JUNE 18.

. . . . . .

Most of the afternoon we were compelled by a storm to spend indoors; and a new chapter was opened at Dulai in our knowledge of Hinduism, for the Swami told us gravely and frankly of its modern abuses and spoke of his own uncompromising hostility to those evil practices which pass under the name of Vâmâchâra.

When we asked how Shri Ramakrishna — who never could bear to condemn the hope of any man — had looked at these things, he told us that "the old man" had said, "Well, well! But every house may have a scavengers' entrance!" And he pointed out that all sects of diabolism in any country belonged to this class. . . .

JUNE 19.

We took it in turns to drive with the Swami in his tonga, and this next day seemed full of reminiscence.

He talked of Brahmavidyâ, the vision of the One, the Alone — Real, and told how love was the only cure for evil. He had had a schoolfellow who grew up and became rich, but lost his health. It was an obscure disease, sapping his energy and vitality daily, yet altogether baffling the skill of the doctors. At last, because he knew that the Swami had always been religious, and men turn to religion when all else fails, he sent to beg him to come to him. When the Master reached him a curious thing happened. There came to his mind a text: "Him the Brahmin conquers who thinks that he is separate from the Brahmin. Him the Kshatriya conquers who thinks that he is separate from the Kshatriya. And him the universe conquers who thinks that he is separate from the universe". And the sick man grasped this and recovered. "And so", said the Swami, "though I often say strange things and angry things, yet remember that in my heart I never seriously mean to preach anything but love! All these things will come right only when we realize that we love each other".

Was it then, or the day before, that talking of the great God, he told us how when he was a child his mother would sigh over his naughtiness and say, "So many prayers and austerities, and instead of a good soul, Shiva has sent me you!" till he was hypnotized into a belief that he was really one of Shiva's demons. He thought that for a punishment he had been banished for a while from Shiva's heaven, and that his one effort in life must be to go back there.

His first act of sacrilege, he told us once, had been committed at the age of five when he embarked on a stormy argument with his mother, to the effect that when his right hand was soiled with eating, it would be cleaner to lift his tumbler of water with the left. For this or similar perversities her most drastic remedy was to put him under the water tap and, while cold water was pouring over his head, to say "Shiva! Shiva!" This, he said, never failed of its effect. The prayer would remind him of his exile, and he would say to himself, "No, no, not this time again!" and so return to quiet and obedience.

He had a surpassing love for Mahâdeva, and once he said of the Indian women of the future that if, amidst their new tasks, they would only remember now and then to say "Shiva! Shiva!" it would be worship enough. The very air of the Himalayas was charged for him with the image of that "eternal meditation" that no thought of pleasure could break. And he understood, he said, for the first time this summer, the meaning of the nature-story that made the Ganges fall on the head of the great God, and wander in and out amongst His matted locks before She found an outlet on the plains below. He had searched long, he said, for the words that the rivers and waterfalls uttered, amongst the mountains, before he had realized that it was the eternal cry "Bom! Bom! Hara! Hara!"

"Yes!" he said of Shiva one day, "He is the great God — calm, beautiful, and silent! And I am His great worshipper".

Again his subject was marriage, as the type of the soul's relation to God. "This is why", he exclaimed, "though the love of a mother is in some ways greater, yet the whole world takes the love of man and woman as the type. *No other has such tremendous idealizing power*. The beloved actually becomes what he is imagined to be. This love transforms its object".

Then the talk strayed to national types, and he spoke of the joy with which the returning traveller greets once more the sight of the men and women of his own country. The whole of life has been a subconscious education to enable one to understand in these every faintest ripple of expression in face and form.

And again we passed a group of Sannyâsins going on foot, and he broke out into fierce invective against asceticism as "savagery" . . . . But the sight of wayfarers doing slow miles on foot in the name of their ideals seemed to rouse in his mind a train of painful associations, and he grew impatient on behalf of humanity at "the torture of religion". Then again the mood passed as suddenly as it had arisen and gave place to the equally strong statement of the conviction that were it not for this "savagery", luxury would have robbed man of all his manliness.

We stopped that evening at Uri Dak bungalow, and in the twilight we all walked in the meadows and the bazaar. How beautiful the place was! A little mud fortress — exactly of the European feudal pattern — overhung the footway as it swept into a great open theatre of field and hill. Along the road above the river lay the bazaar, and we returned to the bungalow by a path across the fields, past cottages in whose gardens the roses were in bloom. As we came, too, it would happen that here and there some child more venturesome than others would play with us.

JUNE 20.

The next day, driving through the most beautiful part of the pass and seeing cathedral rocks and an old ruined temple of the sun, we reached Baramulla. The legend is that the Vale of Kashmir was once a lake and that at this point the Divine Boar pierced the mountains with his tusks and let the Jhelum go free. Another piece of geography in the form of myth. Or is it also prehistoric history?

VI.
The Vale Of Kashmir

PERSONS: The Swami Vivekananda and a party of Europeans and disciples, amongst whom were Dhira Mata, the "Steady Mother"; one whose name was Jaya; and Nivedita.

PLACE: The River Jhelum — Baramulla to Srinagar.

TIME: June 20 to June 22.

"It is said that the Lord Himself is the weight on the side of the fortunate!" cried the Swami in high glee, returning to our room at the Dak bungalow and sitting down with his umbrella on his knees. As he had brought no companion, he had himself to perform all the ordinary little masculine offices, and he had gone out to hire Dungas [houseboats] and do what was necessary. But he had immediately fallen in with a man who, on hearing his name, had undertaken the whole business and sent him back free of responsibility.

So we enjoyed the day. We drank Kashmiri tea out of a Samovar and ate the jam of the country, and at about four o'clock we entered into possession of a flotilla of Dungas, three in number, on which presently we set forth for Srinagar. The first evening, however, we were moored by the garden of the Swami's friend. . . .

We found ourselves next day in the midst of a beautiful valley ringed round with snow mountains. This is known as the Vale of Kashmir, but it might be more accurately described, perhaps, as the Vale of Srinagar. . . .

That first morning, taking a long walk across the fields, we came upon an immense chennaar tree standing in the midst of a wide pasture. It really looked as if the passage through it might shelter the proverbial twenty cows! The Swami fell to architectural visions of how it might be fitted up as a dwelling-place for a hermit. A small cottage might in fact have been built in the hollow of this living tree. And then he talked of meditation, in a way to consecrate every chennaar we should ever see.

We turned with him into the neighbouring farmyard. There we found, seated under a tree, a singularly handsome elderly woman. She wore the crimson coronet and white veil of the Kashmiri wife and sat spinning wool, while round her, helping her, were her two daughters-in-law and their children. The Swami had called at this farm once before in the previous autumn and had often spoken since of the faith and pride of this very woman. He had begged for water, which she had at once given him. Then, before going, he had asked her quietly, "And what, Mother, is your religion?" "I thank God, sir!" had rung out the old voice in pride and triumph. "By the mercy of the Lord, I am a Mussulman!" The whole family received him now as an old friend and were ready to show every courtesy to the friends he had brought.

The journey to Srinagar took two to three days, and one evening, as we walked in the fields before supper, one who had seen the Kalighat complained to the Master of the abandonment of feeling there, which had jarred on her. "*Why* do they kiss the ground before the image?" she exclaimed. The Swami had been pointing to the crop of Til — which he thought to have been the original of the English dill — and calling it "the oldest oil-bearing seed of the Aryans". But at this question he dropped the little blue flower from his hands, and a great hush came over his voice as he stood still and said, "Is it not the same thing to kiss the ground before that image as to kiss the ground before these mountains?"

Our master had promised that before the end of the summer he would take us into retreat and teach us to meditate. . . . It was decided that we should first see the country and afterwards make the retreat.

The first evening in Srinagar we dined out with some Bengali officials, and in the course of conversation one of the Western guests maintained that the history of every nation illustrated and evolved certain ideals to which the people of that nation should hold themselves true. It was very curious to see how the Hindus present objected to this. To them it was clearly a bondage to which the mind of man could not permanently submit itself. Indeed, in their revolt against the fetters of the doctrine, they appeared to be unable to do justice to the idea itself. At last the Swami intervened. "I think you must admit", he said, "that the ultimate unit is psychological. This is much more permanent than the geographical". And then he spoke of cases known to us all, of one of whom he always thought as the most typical "Christian" he had ever seen, yet she was a Bengali woman, and of another, born in the West, who was "a better Hindu than himself". And was not this, after all, the ideal state of things, that each should be born in the other's country to spread the given ideal as far as it could be carried?

VII.
Life At Srinagar

PLACE: Srinagar.

TIME: June 22 to July 15, 1898.

In the mornings we still had long talks as before — some-times it would be the different religious periods through which Kashmir had passed, or the morality of Buddhism, or the history of Shiva-worship, or perhaps the position of Srinagar under Kanishka.

Once he was talking with one of us about Buddhism, and he suddenly said, "The fact is, Buddhism tried to do, in the time of Ashoka, what the world never was ready for till now!" He referred to the federalization of religions. It was a wonderful picture, this, of the religious imperialism of Ashoka, broken down time and again by successive waves of Christianity and Mohammedanism, each claiming exclusive rights over the conscience of mankind and finally to seem to have a possibility, within measurable distance of time, today!

Another time the talk was of Genghis, or Chenghis, Khan, the conqueror from Central Asia. "You hear people talk of him as a vulgar aggressor", he cried passionately, "but that is not true! They are never greedy or vulgar, these great souls! He was inspired with the thought of unity, and he wanted to unify his world. Yes, Napoleon was cast in the same mould. And another, Alexander. Only those three, or perhaps one soul manifesting itself in three different conquests!" And then he passed on to speak of that one soul whom he believed to have come again and again in religion, charged with the divine impulse to bring about the unity of man in God.

At this time the transfer of the *Prabuddha Bharata* from Madras to the newly established Ashrama at Mayavati was much in all our thoughts. The Swami had always had a special love for this paper, as the beautiful name he had given it indicated. He had always been eager too for the establishment of organs of his own. The value of the journal in the education of modern India was perfectly evident to him, and he felt that his master's message and mode of thought required to be spread by this means as well as by preaching and by work. Day after day, therefore, he would dream about the future of his papers, as about the work in its various centres. Day after day he would talk of the forthcoming first number under the new editorship of Swami Swarupananda. And one afternoon he brought to us, as we sat together, a paper on which he said he had "tried to write a letter, but it would come this way!" . . . [*Vide* "To the Awakened India", Complete Works, IV: 387-89]

JUNE 26.

The Master was longing to leave us all and go away into some place of quiet, alone. But we, not knowing this, insisted on accompanying him to the Coloured Springs, called "Kshir Bhavâni", or "Milk of the Mother". It was said to be the first time that Christian or Mohammedan had ever landed there, and we can never be thankful enough for the glimpse we had of it since afterwards it was to become the most sacred of all names to us. . . .

JUNE 29.

Another day we went off quietly by ourselves and visited the Takt-i-Suleiman, a little temple very massively built on the summit of a small mountain two or three thousand feet high. It was peaceful and beautiful, and the famous Floating Gardens could be seen below us for miles around. The Takt-i-Suleiman was one of the great illustrations of the Swami's argument when he would take up the subject of the Hindu love of nature as shown in the choice of sites for temples and architectural monuments. As he had declared, in London, that the saints lived on the hill-tops in order to enjoy the scenery, so now he pointed out — citing one example after another — that our Indian people always consecrated places of peculiar beauty and importance by making there their altars of worship. And there was no denying that the little Takt, crowning the hill that dominated the whole valley, was a case in point.

Many lovely fragments of those days come into mind, as:

> Therefore, Tulasi, take thou care to live with
> all, for who can tell where, or in what garb,
> the Lord Himself may next come to thee?
> One God is hidden in all these, the Torturer
> of all, the Awakener of all, the Reservoir
> of all being, the One who is bereft of all
> qualities.
> There the sun does not shine, nor the moon,
> nor the stars.

There was the story of how Râvana was advised to take the form of Râma in order to cheat Sitâ. He answered, "Have I not thought of it? But in order to take a man's form you must meditate on him; and Rama is the Lord

Himself; so when I meditate on him, even the position of Brahmâ becomes a mere straw. How, then, could I think of a woman?"

"And so", commented the Swami, "even in the commonest or most criminal life, there are these glimpses". It was ever thus. He was constantly interpreting human life as the expression of God, never insisting on the heinousness or wickedness of the act or a character.

"In that which is dark night to the rest of the world, there the man of self-control is awake. That which is life to the rest of the world is sleep to him."

Speaking of Thomas à Kempis one day, and of how he himself used to wander as a Sannyâsin with the Gitâ and the *Imitation* as his whole library, one word, he said, came back to him, inseparably associated with the name of the Western monk:

> Silence! ye teachers of the world, and silence!
> ye prophets! Speak Thou alone, O Lord, unto my soul!

Again:

> The soft Shirisha flower can bear the weight of
> humming bees, but not of birds —
> So Umâ, don't you go and make Tapasyâ!
> Come, Uma, come! delight and idol of my soul!
> Be seated, Mother, on the lotus of my heart,
> And let me take a long, long look at you.
> From my birth up, I am gazing,
> Mother, at your face —
> Know you suffering what trouble,
> and pain?
> Be seated, therefore, Blessed One,
> on the lotus of my heart,
> And dwell there for evermore.

Every now and then there would be long talks about the Gita — "that wonderful poem, without one note in it of weakness or unmanliness." He said one day that it was absurd to complain that knowledge was not given to women or to Shudras. For the whole gist of the Upanishads was contained in the Gita. Without it, indeed, they could hardly be understood; and women and all castes could read the Mahâbhârata.

JULY 4.

With great fun and secrecy the Swami and his one non-American disciple prepared to celebrate the Fourth of July. A regret had been expressed in his hearing that we had no American flag with which to welcome the other members of the party to breakfast on their national festival; and late on the afternoon of the third, he brought a Pundit Durzey [Brahmin tailor] in great excitement, explaining that this man would be glad to imitate it if he were told how. The stars and stripes were very crudely represented, I fear, on the piece of cotton that was nailed with branches of evergreens to the head of the dining—room—boat when the Americans stepped on board for early tea on Independence Day! But the Swami had postponed a journey in order to be present at the little festival, and he himself contributed a poem to the addresses that were now read aloud by way of greeting. . . . [*Vide* "To the Fourth of July", *Complete Works*, V]

JULY 5.

That evening someone pained him by counting the cherry-stones left on her plate, to see when she would be married. He somehow took the play in earnest and came the following morning surcharged with passion for the ideal renunciation.

JULY 6.

"These shadows of home and marriage cross even *my* mind now and then!" he cried, with that tender desire to make himself one with the sinner that he so often showed. But it was across oceans of scorn for those who would glorify the householder that he sought on this occasion to preach the religious life. "Is it so easy", he exclaimed, "to be Janaka? To sit on a throne absolutely unattached? Caring nothing for wealth or fame, for wife or child? One after another in the West has told me that he had reached this. But I could only say, 'Such great men are not born in India'!"

And then he turned to the other side.

"Never forget", he said to one of his hearers, "to say to yourself, and to teach to your children: as is the difference between a firefly and the blazing sun, between the infinite ocean and a little pond, between a mustard-seed and the mountain of Meru, such is the difference between the householder and the Sannyasin!"

"Everything is fraught with fear: Renunciation alone is fearless."

"Blessed be even the fraudulent Sâdhus, and those who have failed to carry out their vows, inasmuch as they also have witnessed to the ideal and so are in some degree the cause of the success of others!"

"Let us never, never, forget our ideal!"

At such moments he would identify himself entirely with the thought he sought to demonstrate, and in the same sense in which a law of nature might be deemed cruel or arrogant, his exposition might have those

qualities. Sitting and listening, we felt ourselves brought face to face with the invisible and absolute.

All this was on our return to Srinagar from the real Fourth of July celebration, which had been a visit to Dahl Lake. . . .

At nine o'clock on the evening of the following Sunday, July the 10th, the first two [Dhira Mata and Jaya] came back unexpectedly, and presently, from many different sources, we gathered the news that the Master had gone to Amarnath by the Sonamarg route and would return another way. He had started out penniless, but that could give no concern to his friends, in a Hindu native state. . . .

JULY 15.

What were we setting out for? We were just moving to go down the river on Friday, and it was close on five in the afternoon when the servants recognized some of their friends in the distance, and word was brought that the Swami's boat was coming towards us.

An hour later he was with us, saying how pleasant it was to be back. The summer had been unusually hot and certain glaciers had given way, rendering the Sonamarg route to Amarnath impracticable. This fact had caused his return.

But from this moment dated the first of three great increments of joy and realization that we saw in him during our months in Kashmir. It was almost as if we could verify for ourselves the truth of that saying of his Guru: "There is indeed a certain ignorance. It has been placed there by my Holy Mother that her work may be done. But it is only like a film of tissue paper. It might be rent at any moment".

VIII.
The Temple Of Pandrenthan

PERSONS: The Swami Vivekananda and a party of Europeans and disciples, amongst whom were Dhira Mata, the "Steady Mother"; one whose name was Jaya; and Nivedita.

PLACE: Kashmir.

TIME: July 16 to 19, 1898.

JULY 16.

It fell to the lot of one of the Swami's disciples next day to go down the river with him in a small boat. As it went, he chanted one song after another of Râmprasâd, and now and again he would translate a verse:

> I call upon thee, Mother.
> For though his mother strikes him,
> The child cries, "Mother! Oh, Mother!"
>
> Though I cannot see Thee,
> I am not a lost child!
> I still cry, "Mother! Mother!"

And then with the haughty dignity of an offended child, some-thing that ended, "I am not the son to call any other woman 'Mother'!"

JULY 17.

It must have been next day that he came into Dhira Mata's Dunga and talked of Bhakti. First it was that curious Hindu thought of Shiva and Umâ in one. It is easy to give the words, but without the voice how comparatively dead they seem! And then there were the wonderful surroundings — picturesque Srinagar, tall Lombardy poplars and distant snows. There in that river-valley, some space from the foot of the great mountains, he chanted to us how "the Lord took a form and that was a divided form, half woman and half man. On one side, beautiful garlands; on the other, bone earrings and coils of snakes. On one side, the hair black, beautiful and in curls; on the other, twisted like rope". And then passing immediately into the other form of the same thought, he quoted:

God became Krishna and Râdhâ —
Love flows in thousands of coils.
Whoso wants, takes it.
Love flows in thousands of coils —
The tide of love and loving past,
And fills the soul with bliss and joy!

So absorbed was he that his breakfast stood unheeded long after it was ready, and when at last he went reluctantly — saying, "When one has all this Bhakti what does one want with food?"— it was only to come back again quickly and resume the subject.

But either now or at some other time he said that he did not talk of Radha and Krishna where he looked for deeds. It was Shiva who made stern and earnest workers, and to Him the labourer must be dedicated.

The next day he gave us a quaint saying of Shri Ramakrishna, comparing the critics of others to bees or flies, according as they chose honey or wounds.

And then we were off to Islamabad, and really, as it proved, to Amarnath.

JULY 19.

The first afternoon, in a wood by the side of the Jhelum, we discovered the long — sought temple of Pandrenthan (Pandresthan, place of the Pândavas?).

It was sunk in a pond, and this was thickly covered with scum out of which it rose, a tiny cathedral of the long ago, built of heavy grey limestone. The temple consisted of a small cell with four doorways opening to the cardinal points. Externally it was a tapering pyramid — with its top truncated, to give foot-hold to a bush — supported on a four-pierced pedestal. In its architecture, trefoil and triangular arches were combined in an unusual fashion with each other and with the straight-lined lintel. It was built with marvellous solidity, and the necessary lines were somewhat obscured by heavy ornament. . . .

For all but the Swami himself, this was our first peep at Indian archaeology. So when he had been through it, he taught us how to observe the interior.

In the centre of the ceiling was a large sun-medallion, set in a square whose points were the points of the compass. This left four equal triangles at the corners of the ceiling, which were filled with sculpture in low relief, male and female figures intertwined with serpents, beautifully done. On the wall were empty spaces, where seemed to have been a band of topes.

Outside, carvings were similarly distributed. In one of the trefoil arches — over, I think, the eastern door — was a fine image of the Teaching Buddha, standing, with his hand uplifted. Running round the buttresses was a much-defaced frieze of a seated woman with a tree — evidently Mâyâ Devi, the mother of Buddha. The three other door-niches were empty, but a slab by the pond-side seemed to have fallen from one, and this contained a bad figure of a king, said by the country-people to represent the sun.

The masonry of this little temple was superb and probably accounted for its long preservation. A single block of stone would be so cut as to correspond not to one brick in a wall, but to a section of the architect's plan. It would turn a corner and form part of two distinct walls, or sometimes even of three. This fact made one take the building as very, very old, possibly even earlier than Marttanda. The theory of the workmen seemed so much more that of carpentering than of building! The water about it was probably an overflow into the temple-court from the sacred spring that the chapel itself may have been placed, as the Swami thought, to enshrine.

To him, the place was delightfully suggestive. It was a direct memorial of Buddhism, representing one of the four religious periods into which he had already divided the history of Kashmir: (1) tree and snake worship, from which dated all the names of the springs ending in Nag, as Verinag, and so on; (2) Buddhism; (3) Hinduism, in the form of sun worship; and (4) Mohammedanism.

Sculpture, he told us, was the characteristic art of Buddhism, and the sun-medallion, or lotus, one of its commonest ornaments. The figures with the serpents referred to pre-Buddhism. But sculpture had greatly deteriorated under sun worship, hence the crudity of the Surya figure. . . .

It was the time of sunset — such a sunset! The mountains in the west were all a shimmering purple. Further north they were blue with snow and cloud. The sky was green and yellow and touched with red — bright flame and daffodil colours, against a blue and opal background. We stood and looked, and then the Master, catching sight of the throne of Solomon — that little Takt which we already loved — exclaimed, "What genius the Hindu shows in placing his temples! He always chooses a grand scenic effect! See! The Takt commands the whole of Kashmir. The rock of Hari Parbat rises red out of blue water, like a lion couchant, crowned. And the temple of Marttanda has the valley at its feet!"

Our boats were moored near the edge of the wood, and we could see that the presence of the silent chapel, of the Buddha, which we had just explored, moved the Swami deeply. That evening we all foregathered in Dhira Mata's houseboat, and a little of the conversation has been noted down.

Our master had been talking of Christian ritual as derived from Buddhist, but one of the party would have none of the theory.

"Where did Buddhist ritual itself come from?" she asked.

"From Vedic", answered the Swami briefly."

Or as it was present also in southern Europe, is it not better to suppose a common origin for it and the Christian and the Vedic rituals?"

"No! No!" he replied. "You forget that Buddhism was entirely within Hinduism! Even caste was not attacked — it was not yet crystallized, of course! — and Buddha merely tried to restore the ideal. *He who attains to God in this life,* says Manu, *is the Brahmin.* Buddha would have had it so, if he could."

"But how are Vedic and Christian rituals connected?" persisted his opponent. "How could they be the same? You have nothing even corresponding to the central rite of our worship!"

"Why, yes!" said the Swami. "Vedic ritual has its Mass, the offering of food to God; your Blessed Sacrament, our Prasâdam. Only it is offered sitting, not kneeling, as is common in hot countries. They kneel in Tibet. Then too Vedic ritual has its lights, incense, music."

"But", was the somewhat ungracious argument, "has it any common prayer?" Objections urged in this way always elicited some bold paradox which contained a new and unthought-of generalization.

He flashed down on the question. "No! And neither has Christianity! That is pure Protestantism and Protestantism took it from the Mohammedans, perhaps through Moorish influence!

"Mohammedanism is the only religion that has completely broken down the idea of the priest. The leader of prayer stands with his back to the people, and only the reading of the Koran may take place from the pulpit. Protestantism is an approach to this.

"Even the tonsure existed in India, in the shaven head. I have seen a picture of Justinian receiving the Law from two monks, in which the monks' heads are entirely shaven. The monk and nun both existed in pre-Buddhistic Hinduism. Europe gets her orders from the Thebaid."

"At that rate, then, you accept Catholic ritual as Aryan!"

"Yes, almost all Christianity is Aryan, I believe. I am inclined to think Christ never existed. I have doubted that ever since I had my dream — that dream off Crete! Indian and Egyptian ideas met at Alexandria and went forth to the world, tinctured with Judaism and Hellenism, as Christianity.

"The Acts and Epistles, you know, are older than the Gospels, and S. John is spurious. The only figure we can be sure of is S. Paul, and he was not an eye-witness, and according to his own showing was capable of Jesuitry — 'by all means save souls' — isn't it?

"No! Buddha and Mohammed, alone amongst religious teachers, stand out with historic distinctness — having been fortunate enough to have, while they were living, enemies as well as friends. Krishna — I doubt; a Yogi, a shepherd, and a great king have all been amalgamated in one beautiful figure, holding the Gitâ in his hand.

"Renan's life of Jesus is mere froth. It does not touch Strauss, the real antiquarian. Two things stand out as personal living touches in the life of Christ — the woman taken in adultery, the most beautiful story in literature, and the woman at the well. How strangely true is this last to Indian life! A woman coming to draw water finds, seated at the well-side, a yellow-clad monk. He asks her for water. Then he teaches her and does a little mind-reading and so on. Only in an Indian story, when she went to call the villagers to look and listen, the monk would have taken his chance and fled to the forest!

"On the whole, I think old Rabbi Hillel is responsible for the teachings of Jesus, and an obscure Jewish sect of Nazarenes — a sect of great antiquity — suddenly galvanized by S. Paul, furnished the mythic personality as a centre of worship.

"The resurrection, of course, is simply spring-cremation. Only the rich Greeks and Romans had had cremation anyway, and the new sun-myth would only stop it amongst the few.

"But Buddha! Buddha! Surely he was the greatest man who ever lived. He never drew a breath for himself. Above all, he never claimed worship. He said, 'Buddha is not a man, but a state. I have found the door. Enter, all of you!'

"He went to the feast of Ambâpâli, 'the sinner'. He dined with the pariah, though he knew it would kill him, and sent a message to his host on his death-bed, thanking him for the great deliverance. Full of love and pity for a little goat, even before he had attained the truth! You remember how he offered his own head, that of prince and monk, if only the king would spare the kid that he was about to sacrifice, and how the king was so struck by his compassion that he saved its life? Such a mixture of rationalism and feeling was never seen! Surely, surely, there was none like him!"

IX.
Walks And Talks Beside The Jhelum

PERSONS: The Swami Vivekananda and a party of Europeans and disciples, amongst whom were Dhira Mata, the "Steady Mother"; one whose name was Jaya; and Nivedita.

PLACE: Kashmir.

TIME: July 20 to July 29, 1898.

JULY 20.

. . . . . .

That morning the river was broad and shallow and clear, and two of us walked with the Swami across the fields and along the banks about three miles. He began by talking of the sense of sin, how it was Egyptian, Semitic and Aryan. It appears in the Vedas, but quickly passes out. The devil is recognized there as the Lord of Anger. Then, with the Buddhists he became Mara, the Lord of Lust, and one of the most loved of the Lord Buddha's titles was "Conqueror of Mara". (*Vide* the Sanskrit lexicon Amarkosha that Swami learnt to patter as a child of four!) But while Satan is the Hamlet of the Bible, in the Hindu scriptures the Lord of Anger never divides creation. He always represents defilement, never duality.

Zoroaster was a reformer of some old religion. Even Ormuzd and Ahriman with him were not supreme; they were only manifestations of the Supreme. That older religion must have been Vedantic. So the Egyptians and Semites cling to the theory of sin while the Aryans, as Indians and Greeks, quickly lose it. In India righteousness and sin become Vidyâ and Avidyâ — both to be transcended. Amongst the Aryans, Persians and Europeans become Semitized by religious ideas; hence the sense of sin.

And then the talk drifted, as it was always so apt to do, to questions of the country and the future. What idea must be urged on a people to give them strength? The line of their own development runs in one way, A. Must the new accession of force be a compensating one, B? This would produce a development midway between the two, C — a geometrical alteration merely. But it was not so.

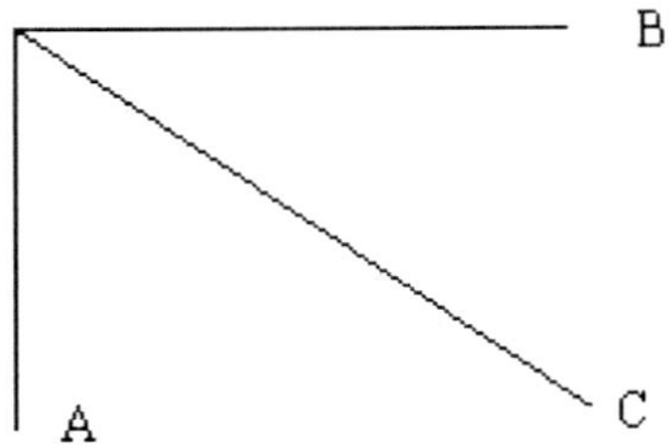

National life was a question of organic forces. We must reinforce the current of that life itself, and leave it to do the rest. Buddha preached renunciation, and India heard. Yet within a thousand years she had reached her highest point of national prosperity. The national life in India has renunciation as its source. Its highest ideals are service and Mukti. The Hindu mother eats last. Marriage is not for individual happiness, but for the welfare of the nation and the caste. Certain individuals of the modern reform, having embarked on an experiment which could not solve the problem, "are the sacrifices over which the race has to walk".

And then the trend of conversation changed again and became all fun and merriment, jokes and stories. And as we laughed and listened, the boats came up and talk was over for the day.

The whole of that afternoon and night the Swami lay in his boat, ill. But next day, when we landed at the temple of Bijbehara — already thronged with Amarnath pilgrims — he was able to join us for a little while. "Quickly up and quickly down", as he said of himself, was always his characteristic. After that he was with us most of the day, and in the afternoon we reached Islamabad. . . .

In the dusk that evening one came into the little group amongst the apple trees and found the Master engaged in the rarest of rare happenings, a personal talk with Dhira Mata and her whose name was Jaya. He had taken two pebbles into his hand and was saying how, when he was well, his mind might direct itself to this and that, or his will might seem less firm; but let the least touch of pain or illness come, let him look death in the face for a while, and "I am as hard as that (knocking the stones together), for I *have* touched the feet of God".

And one remembered, apropos of this coolness, the story of a walk across the fields in England, where he and an Englishman and woman had been pursued by an angry bull. The Englishman frankly ran and reached the other side of the hill in safety. The woman ran as far as she could and then sank to the ground, incapable of further effort. Seeing this, and unable to aid her, the Swami — thinking "So *this* is the end, after all" — took up his stand in front of her, with folded arms. He told afterwards how his mind was occupied with a mathematical calculation as to how far the bull would be able to throw. But the animal suddenly stopped a few paces off and then, raising his head, retreated sullenly.

A like courage — though he himself was far from thinking of these incidents — had shown itself in his early youth when he quietly stepped up to a runaway horse and caught it in the streets of Calcutta, thus saving the life of the woman who occupied the carriage behind.

The talk drifted on, as we sat on the grass beneath the trees, and became, for an hour or two, half grave, half gay. We heard much of the tricks the monkeys could play in Vrindaban. And we elicited stories of two separate occasions in his wandering life when he had had clear previsions of help which had been fulfilled. One of these I remember. It may possibly have occurred at the time when he was under the vow to ask for nothing, and he had been several days (perhaps five) without food. Suddenly, as he lay almost dying of exhaustion in a railway-station, it flashed into his mind that he must rise up and go out along a certain road and that there he would meet a man bringing him help. He obeyed and met one carrying a tray of food. "Are you he to whom I was sent?" said this man, coming up to him and looking at him closely.

Then a child was brought to us, with its hand badly cut, and the Swami applied an old wives' cure. He bathed the wound with water and then laid on it, to stop the bleeding, the ashes of a piece of calico. The villagers were soothed and consoled, and our gossip was over for the evening.

JULY 23.

The next morning a motley gathering of coolies assembled beneath the apple-trees and waited some hours to take us to the ruins of Marttanda. It had been a wonderful old building — evidently more abbey than temple — in a wonderful position; and its great interest lay in the obvious agglomeration of styles and periods in which it had grown up. . . . Its presence is a perpetual reminder that the East was the original home of monasticism. The Swami was hard at work in an instant on observations and theories, pointing out the cornice that ran along the nave from the entrance to the sanctuary, to the west, surmounted by the high trefoils of the two arches and also by a frieze; or showing us the panels containing cherubs; and before we had done, had picked up a couple of coins. The ride back through the sunset light was charming. From all these hours, the day before and the day after, fragments of talk come back to me.

"No nation, not Greek or another, has ever carried patriotism so far as the Japanese. They don't talk, they act — give up all for country. There are noblemen now living in Japan as peasants, having given up their princedoms without a word to create the unity of the empire. And not one traitor could be found in the Japanese war. Think of that!"

Again, talking of the inability of some to express feeling, "Shy and reserved people, I have noticed, are always the most brutal when roused".

Again, evidently talking of the ascetic life and giving the rules of Brahmacharya — "The Sannyâsin who thinks of gold, to desire it, commits suicide", and so on.

JULY 24.

The darkness of night and the forest, a great pine-fire under the trees, two or three tents standing out white in the blackness, the forms and voices of many servants at their fires in the distance, and the Master with three disciples, such is the next picture. . . . Suddenly the Master turned to one member of the party and said, "You never mention your school now. Do you sometimes forget it? You see", he went on, "I have much to think of. One day I turn to Madras and think of the work there. Another day I give all my attention to America or England or Ceylon or Calcutta. Now I am thinking about yours".

At that moment the Master was called away to dine, and not till he came back could the confidence he had invited be given.

He listened to it all, the deliberate wish for a tentative plan, for smallness of beginnings, and the final inclination to turn away from the idea of inclusiveness and breadth and to base the whole of an educational effort on the religious life and on the worship of Shri Ramakrishna.

"Because you must be sectarian to get that enthusiasm, must you not?" he said. "You will make a sect in order to rise above all sects. Yes I understand".

There would be obvious difficulties. The thing sounded on this scale almost impossible for many reasons. But for the moment the only care need be to will rightly; and if the plan was sound, ways and means would be found to hand, that was sure.

He waited a little when he had heard it all, and then he said, "You ask me to criticize, but that I cannot do. For I regard you as inspired, quite as much inspired as I am. You know that's the difference between other religions and us. Other people believe their founder was inspired, and so do we. But so am I also, just as much so as he, and you as I; and after you, your girls and their disciples will be. So I shall help you to do what you think best".

Then he turned to Dhira Mata and to Jaya and spoke of the greatness of the trust that he would leave in the hands of that disciple who should represent the interests of women when he should go West, of how it would exceed the responsibility of work for men. And he added, turning to the worker of the party, "Yes, you have faith, but you have not that burning enthusiasm that you need. You want to be consumed [with] energy. Shiva! Shiva!" And so, invoking the blessing of Mahâdeva, he said goodnight and left us, and we presently went to bed.

JULY 25.

The next morning we breakfasted early in one of the tents and went on to Achhabal. One of us had had a dream of old jewels lost and restored, all bright and new. But the Swami, smiling, stopped the tale, saying, "Never talk of a dream as good as that!"

At Achhabal we found more gardens of Jehangir. Was it here or at Verinag that had been his favourite resting-place?

We roamed about the gardens and bathed in a still pool opposite the Pathan Khan's Zenana, and then we lunched in the first garden and rode down in the afternoon to Islamabad.

As we sat at lunch, the Swami invited his daughter to go to the cave of Amarnath with him and be dedicated to Shiva. Dhira Mata smiled permission, and the next half-hour was given to pleasure and congratulations. It had already been arranged that we were all to go to Pahalgam and wait there for the Swami's return from the pilgrimage. So we reached the boats that evening, packed and wrote letters, and next day in the afternoon started for Bawan.

X.
The Shrine Of Amarnath

PLACE: Kashmir.

TIME: July 29 to August 8, 1898.

JULY 29.

From this time we saw very little of the Swami. He was full of enthusiasm about the pilgrimage and lived mostly on one meal a day, seeking no company much, save that of Sâdhus. Sometimes he would come to a camping-ground, beads in hand. Tonight two of the party went roaming about Bawan, which was like a village fair, all modified by a religious tendency centering in the sacred springs. Afterwards with Dhira Mata it was possible to go and listen at the tent door to the crowd of Hindi-speaking Sadhus who were plying the Swami with questions.

On Thursday we reached Pahalgam and camped down at the lower end of the valley. We found that the Swami had to encounter high opposition over the question of our admission at all. He was supported by the Naked Swamis, one of whom said, "It is true you have this strength, Swamiji, but you ought not to manifest it!" He yielded at the word. That afternoon, however, he took his daughter round the camp to be blessed, which really meant to distribute alms — and whether because he was looked upon as rich or because he was recognized as strong, the next day our tents were moved up to a lovely knoll at the head of the camp. . . .

JULY 30.

. . . . . .

How beautiful was the route to the next halt, Chandanwari! There we camped on the edge of a ravine. It rained all afternoon, and I was visited by the Swami only for a five-minutes' chat. But I received endless touching little kindnesses from the servants and other pilgrims. . . .

. . . Close to Chandanwari the Swami insisted on my doing my first glacier on foot and took care to point out every detail of interest. A tremendous climb of some thousands of feet was the next experience. Then a long walk along a narrow path that twisted round mountain after mountain, and finally another steep climb. At the top of the first mountain, the ground was simply carpeted with edelweiss. Then the road passed five hundred feet above Sheshnag with its sulky water, and at last we camped in a cold damp place amongst the snow-peaks, 18,000 feet high. The firs were far below, and all afternoon and evening the coolies had to forage for juniper in all directions. The Tahsildar's, Swami's and my own tents were all close together, and in the evening a large fire was lighted in front. But it did not burn well, and many feet below lay the glacier. I did not see the Swami after we camped.

Panchatarani — the place of the five streams — was not nearly such a long march. Moreover, it was lower than Sheshnag, and the cold was dry and exhilarating. In front of the camp was a dry riverbed, all gravel, and through this ran five streams, in all of which it was the duty of the pilgrim to bathe, walking from one to the other in wet garments. Contriving to elude observation completely, Swamiji nevertheless fulfilled the law to the last letter in this respect. . . .

At these heights we often found ourselves in great circles of snow-peaks, those mute giants that have suggested to the Hindu mind the idea of the ash-encovered God.

AUGUST 2.

On Tuesday, August the 2nd, the great day of Amarnath, the first batch of pilgrims must have left the camp at two! We left by the light of the full moon. The sun rose as we went down the narrow valley. It was not too safe at this part of the journey. But when we left our Dandies and began to climb, the real danger began. . . . Then, having at last reached the bottom of the farther slope, we had to toil along the glacier mile after mile to the cave. . . .

The Swami, exhausted, had by this time fallen behind. . . . He came at last and with a word sent me on; he was going to bathe. Half an hour later he entered the cave. With a smile he knelt first at one end of the semi-circle, then at the other. The place was vast, large enough to hold a cathedral; and the great ice-Shiva, in a niche of deepest shadow, seemed as if throned on its own base. A few minutes passed, and then he turned to leave the cave.

To him, the heavens had opened. He had touched the feet of Shiva. He had had to hold himself tight, he said afterwards, lest he "should swoon away". But so great was his physical exhaustion that a doctor said afterwards that his heart ought to have stopped beating, but had undergone a permanent enlargement instead. How strangely near fulfilment had been those words of his Master, "When he realizes who and what he is, he will give up this body!"

"I have enjoyed it so much!" he said half an hour afterwards, as he sat on a rock above the stream-side, eating lunch with the kind Naked Swami and me. "I thought the ice Linga was Shiva Himself. And there were no thievish Brahmins, no trade, nothing wrong. It was all worship. I never enjoyed any religious place so much!"

Afterwards he would often tell of the overwhelming vision that had seemed to draw him almost into its vertex. He would talk of the poetry of the white ice-pillar; and it was he who suggested that the first discovery of the place had been by a party of shepherds, who had wandered far in search of their flocks one summer day and had entered the cave to find themselves before the unmelting ice, in the presence of the Lord Himself. He always said too that the grace of Amarnath had been granted to him there, not to die till he himself should give consent. And to me he said, "You do not now understand. But you have made the pilgrimage, and it will go on working. Causes must bring their effects. You will understand better afterwards. The effects will come".

How beautiful was the road by which we returned next morning to Pahalgam! We struck tents that night immediately on our return to them and camped later for the night in a snowy pass a whole stage further on. We paid a coolie a few annas here to push on with a letter; but when we actually arrived next afternoon we found that this had been quite unnecessary, for all morning long relays of pilgrims had been passing the tents and dropping in, in the most friendly manner, to give the others news of us and our impending arrival. In the morning we were up and on the way long before dawn. As the sun rose before us, while the moon went down behind, we passed above the Lake of Death, into which about forty pilgrims had been buried one year by an avalanche which their hymns had started. After this we came to the tiny goat-path down the face of a steep cliff by which we were able to shorten the return journey so much. This was little better than a scramble, and everyone had perforce to do it on foot. At the bottom the villagers had something like breakfast ready. Fires were burning, Chapatties baking, and tea was ready to be served out. From this time on parties of pilgrims would leave the main body at each parting of the ways, and the feeling of solidarity that had grown up amongst us all throughout the journey became gradually less and less.

That evening on the knoll above Pahalgam, where a great fire of pine-logs was lighted and Dhurries spread, we all sat and talked. Our friend

the Naked Swami joined us and we had plenty of fun and nonsense, but presently, when all had gone save our own little party, we sat on with the great moon overhead and the towering snows and rushing rivers and the mountain-pines. And the Swami talked of Shiva and the cave and the great verge of vision.

AUGUST 8.

We started for Islamabad next day, and on Monday morning as we sat at breakfast, we were towed safely into Srinagar.

XI.
At Srinagar On The Return Journey

PERSONS: The Swami Vivekananda and a party of Europeans and disciples, amongst whom were Dhira Mata, the "Steady Mother"; one whose name was Jaya; and Nivedita.

PLACE: Kashmir — Srinagar.

TIME: August 9 to August 13, 1898.

AUGUST 9.

At this time the Master was always talking of leaving us. And when I find the entry "The river is pure that flows, the monk is pure that goes", I know exactly what it means — the passionate outcry "I am always so much better when I have to undergo hardships and beg my bread", the longing for freedom and the touch of the common people, the picture of himself making a long circuit of the country on foot and meeting us again at Baramulla for the journey home.

His family of boat-people, whom he had staunchly befriended through two seasons, left us today. Afterwards he would refer to the whole incident of their connection with him as proof that even charity and patience could go too far.

AUGUST 10.

It was evening, and we all went out to pay some visit. On the return he called his disciple Nivedita to walk with him across the fields. His talk was all about the work and his intentions in it. He spoke of the inclusiveness of his conception of the country and its religions; of his own distinction as being solely in his desire to make Hinduism active, aggressive, a missionary faith; of "don't-touch-ism" as the only thing he repudiated. Then he talked with depth of feeling of the gigantic spirituality of many of those who were most orthodox. India wanted practicality, but she must never let go her hold on the old meditative life for that. "To be as deep as the ocean and as broad as the sky", Shri Ramakrishna has said, was the ideal. But this profound inner life in the soul encased within orthodoxy is the result of an accidental, not an essential, association. "And if we set ourselves right here, the world will be right, for are we not all one? Ramakrishna Paramahamsa was alive to the depths of his being, yet on the outer plane he was perfectly active and capable."

And then of that critical question of the worship of his own master, "My own life is guided by the enthusiasm of that great personality, but others will decide for themselves how far this is true for them. Inspiration is not filtered out to the world through one man".

AUGUST 11.

There was occasion this day for the Swami to rebuke a member of this party for practising palmistry. It was a thing he said that everyone desired, yet all India despised and hated. Yes, he said, in reply to a little special pleading, even of character-reading he disapproved. "To tell you the truth, I should have thought even your incarnation more honest if he and his disciples had not performed miracles. Buddha unfrocked a monk for doing it." Later, talking on the subject to which he had now transferred his attention, he spoke with horror of the display of the least of it as sure to bring a terrible reflex.

AUGUST 12 AND 13.

The Swami had now taken a Brahmin cook. Very touching had been the arguments of the Amarnath Sâdhus against his willingness to let even a Mussulman cook for him. "Not in the land of Sikhs at least, Swamiji", they had said, and he had at last consented. But for the present he was worshipping his little Mohammedan boat-child as Umâ. Her whole idea of love was service, and the day he left Kashmir she, tiny one, was fain to carry a tray of apples for him all the way to the tonga herself. He never forgot her, though he seemed quite indifferent at the time. In Kashmir itself he was fond of recalling the time when she saw a blue flower on the towing path and sitting down before it, and striking it this way and that, "was alone with that flower for twenty minutes".

There was a piece of land by the riverside on which grew three chennaars, towards which our thoughts turned with peculiar love at this time. For the Mahârâjâ was anxious to give it to Swamiji, and we all pictured it as a centre of work in the future — work which should realize the great idea of "by the people, for the people, as a joy to worker and to served".

In view of Indian feeling about a homestead blessed by women, it had been suggested that we should go and annex the site by camping there for a while. One of our party, moreover, had a personal wish for special quiet at this time. So it was decided that we should establish "a women's Math", as it were, before the Maharaja should require the land to confer it on the Swami. And this was possible because the spot was one of the minor camping grounds used by Europeans.

XII.
The Camp Under The Chennaars

PERSONS: The Swami Vivekananda and a party of Europeans and disciples, amongst whom were Dhira Mata, the "Steady Mother"; one whose name was Jaya; and Nivedita.

PLACE: Kashmir — Srinagar.

TIME: August 14 to August 20, 1898.

AUGUST 14.

It was Sunday morning and next afternoon the Swami was prevailed on to come up to tea with us in order to meet a European guest who seemed to be interested in the subject of Vedanta. He had been little inclined to concern himself with the matter, and I think his real motive in accepting was probably to afford his too-eager disciples an opportunity of convincing themselves of the utter futility of all such attempts as this. Certainly he took infinite pains with the enquirer and, as certainly, his trouble was wasted.

I remember his saying, amongst other things, "How I wish a law could be broken. If we were really able to break a law we should be free. What you call breaking the law is really only another way of keeping it". Then he tried to explain a little of the superconscious life. But his words fell on ears that could not hear.

AUGUST 16.

On Tuesday he came once more to our little camp to the midday meal. Towards the end it began to rain heavily enough to prevent his return, and he took up Tod's*History of Rajasthan*, which was lying near, and drifted into talk of Mirâ Bâi. "Two-thirds of the national ideas now in Bengal", he said, "have been gathered from this book".

But the episode of Mira Bai, the queen who would not be queen, but would wander the world with the lovers of Krishna, was always his favourite, even in Tod. He talked of how she preached submission, prayerfulness, and service to all in contrast to Chaitanya, who preached love to the name of God, and mercy to all.

Mira Bai was always one of his great patronesses. He would put into her story many threads with which one is now familiar in other connections, such as the conversation of two great robbers, and the end by an image of Krishna opening and swallowing her up. I heard him on one occasion recite and translate one of her songs to a woman. I wish I could remember the whole, but it began in his rendering with the words "Cling to it, cling to it, cling to it, Brother", and ended with "If Ankâ and Bankâ, the robber brothers; Sujan, the fell butcher; and the courtesan who playfully taught her parrot to repeat the name of the Lord Krishna were saved, there is hope for all".

Again, I have heard him tell that marvellous tale of Mira Bai in which on reaching Vrindaban, she sent for a certain famous Sâdhu. He refused to go on the ground that women might not see men in Vrindaban. When this had happened three times, Mira Bai went to him herself saying that she had not known that there were such beings as men there; she had supposed that Krishna alone existed. And when she saw the astonished Sadhu, she unveiled herself completely, with the words "Fool, do you call yourself a man?" And as he fell prostrate before her with a cry of awe, she blessed him as a mother blesses her child.

Today the Swami passed on to the talk of Akbar and sang us a song of Tânsen, the poet-laureate of the emperor:

Seated on the throne, a god amongst men,
Thou, the Emperor of Delhi.
Blessed was the hour, the minute, the second,
When thou ascendest the throne,
O God amongst men,
Thou, the Lord of Delhi.
Long live thy crown, thy sceptre, thy throne,
O God amongst men,
Thou, Emperor of Delhi.
Live long, and remain awakened always,
O son of Humayoon,
Joy of the sun, God amongst men,
Thou, the Emperor of Delhi!

Then the talk passed to "our national hero" Pratâp Singh, who never could be brought to submission. Once indeed he was tempted to give in, at that moment when having fled from Chitore and the queen herself having cooked the scanty evening meal, a hungry cat swooped down on that cake of bread which was the children's portion, and the King of Mewar heard his babies cry for food. Then, indeed, the strong heart of the man failed him. The prospect of ease and relief tempted him. And for a moment he thought of ceasing from the unequal conflict and sending his alliance to Akbar, only for an instant. The Eternal Will protects its own. Even as the picture passed before his mind, there appeared a messenger with those despatches from a famous Rajput chief that said, "There is but one left amongst us who has kept his blood free from admixture with the alien. Let it never be said that his head has touched the dust". And the soul of Pratap drew in the long breath of courage and renewed faith; and he arose and swept the country of its foes and made his own way back to Udaipur.

Then there was the wonderful tale of the virgin princess Krishna Kumâri, whose hand was sought by various royal suitors at once. And when three armies were at the gate, her father could think of nothing better than to give her poison. The task was entrusted to her uncle, and he entered her room, as she lay asleep, to do it. But at the sight of her beauty and youth, remembering her too as a baby, the soldier's heart failed him, and he could not perform his task. But she was awakened by some sound, and being told what was proposed, stretched out her hand for the cup and drank the poison with a smile. And so on, and so on. For the stories of Rajput heroes in this kind are endless.

AUGUST 20.

On Saturday the Swami and he whose name was Soong went to the Dahl Lake to be the guests of the American consul and his wife for a couple of days. They returned on Monday, and on Tuesday the Swami came up to the new Math, as we called it, and had his boat moved close by ours so that he could be with us for a few days before leaving for Ganderbal.

Concluding Words Of The Editor

From Ganderbal the Swami returned by the first week of October and announced his intention of leaving for the plains in a few days for urgent reasons. The European party had already made plans to visit the principal cities of northern India, e.g., Lahore, Delhi, Agra, etc., as soon as the winter set in. So both parties decided to return together and came to Lahore. From here the Swami and his party returned to Calcutta, leaving the rest to carry out their plans for sight-seeing in northern India.

Sayings and Utterances

List Of Abbreviations

In this section, only Swami Vivekananda's direct words have been placed within quotation marks. References have been identified by the following abbreviations:

ND Burke, Marie Louise. *Swami Vivekananda in the West: New Discoveries*. 6 vols. Calcutta: Advaita Ashrama, 1983-87.

CWSN Nivedita, Sister. *The Complete Works of Sister Nivedita*. Vol. 1. Calcutta: Advaita Ashrama, 1982.

LSN Nivedita, Sister. *Letters of Sister Nivedita*. 2 vols. Compiled and edited by Sankari Prasad Basu. Calcutta: Nababharat Publishers, 1982.

VIN Basu, Sankari Prasad and Ghosh, Sunil Bihari, eds. *Vivekananda in Indian Newspapers:* 1893-1902. Calcutta: Dineshchandra Basu, Basu Bhattacharya and Co., 1969.

1. *From Mrs. Prince Woods's description of Swami Vivekananda's departure from the Woods's residence in Salem, Massachusetts, in August 1893. Swami Vivekananda gave his staff, his most precious possession, to Dr. Woods, who was at that time a young medical student, and his trunk and his blanket to Mrs. Kate T. Woods, saying:*

"Only my most precious possessions should I give to my friends who have made me at home in this great country." (*ND* 1: 42)

2. *On the back of Swami Vivekananda's transcription from Louis Rousselet's book India and Its Native Princes — Travels in Central India and in the Presidencies of Bombay and Bengal, dated February 11, 1894:*

"I say there is but one remedy for one too anxious for the future — to go down on his knees." (*ND* 1: 225)

3. *An extract from a prayer Swami Vivekananda delivered at the Chicago World's Parliament of Religions:*

"Thou art He that beareth the burdens of the universe; help me to bear the little burden of this life." (*ND* 2: 32)

4. An extract from another prayer offered by Swami Vivekananda at the Chicago World's Parliament of Religions:

"At the head of all these laws, in and through every particle of matter and force, stands One through whose command the wind blows, the fire burns, the clouds rain, and death stalks upon the earth. And what is His nature? He is everywhere the pure and formless One, the Almighty and the All Merciful. Thou art our Father. Thou art our beloved Friend." (*ND* 2: 33)

5. From Mary T. Wright's journal entry dated Saturday, May 12, 1894:

The widows of high caste in India do not marry, he said; only the widows of low caste may marry, may eat, drink, dance, have as many husbands as they choose, divorce them all, in short enjoy all the benefits of the highest society in this country. . . .

"*When we* are fanatical", he said, "we torture ourselves, we throw ourselves under huge cars, we cut our throats, we lie on spiked beds; but when *you* are fanatical you cut other people's throats, you torture them by fire and put *them* on spiked beds! You take very good care of your own skins!" (*ND* 2: 58-59)

6. An 1894 extract from the Greenacre Voice, quoting one of the Swami's teachings delivered at Greenacre, Maine:

"You and I and everything in the universe are that Absolute, not parts, but the whole. You are the whole of that Absolute." (*ND* 2: 150)

7. In a March 5, 1899 letter from Sister Nivedita to Miss Josephine MacLeod:

"I am at heart a mystic, Margot, all this reasoning is only apparent — I am really always on the lookout for signs and things — and so I never bother about the fate of my initiations. If they want to be Sannyâsins badly enough I feel that the rest is not my business. Of course it has its bad side. I have to pay dearly for my blunder sometimes — but it has one advantage. It has kept me still a Sannyasin through all this — and that is my ambition, to die a real Sannyasin as Ramakrishna Paramahamsa actually was — free from lust — and desire of wealth, and thirst for fame. That thirst for fame is the worst of all filth." (*ND* 3: 128-29)

8. From John Henry Wright's March 27, 1896 letter to Mary Tappan Wright, in which Swami Vivekananda stated that England is just like India with its castes:

"I had to have separate classes for the two castes. For the high caste people — Lady This and Lady That, Honourable This and Honourable That — I had classes in the morning; for the low caste people, who came pell-mell, I had classes in the evening." (*ND* 4: 73)

9. While Swami Vivekananda was offering flowers at the feet of the Virgin Mary in a small chapel in Switzerland in the summer of 1896, he said:

"For she also is the Mother." (*ND* 4: 276)

10. From Mr. J. J. Goodwin's October 23, 1896 letter to Mrs. Ole Bull, quoting Swami Vivekananda's conversation at Greycoat Gardens in London

"It is very good to have a high ideal, but don't make it too high. A high ideal raises mankind, but an impossible ideal lowers them from the very impossibility of the case." (*ND* 4: 385)

11. A November 20, 1896 entry from Swami Abhedananda's diary, quoting Swami Vivekananda's observation of the English people:

"You can't make friends here without knowing their customs, behaviour, politics. You have to know the manners of the rich, the cultured and the poor." (*ND* 4: 478)

12. In Mr. J. J. Goodwin's November 11, 1896 letter to Mrs. Ole Bull, quoting Swami Vivekananda's unpublished statement toward the end of "Practical Vedanta — IV":

"A Jiva can never attain absolutely to Brahman until the whole of Mâyâ disappears. While there is still a Jiva left in Maya, there can be no soul absolutely free. . . . Vedantists are divided on this point." (*ND* 4: 481)

13. From Swami Saradananda's letter to a brother-disciple, concerning Swami Vivekananda's last days:

Sometimes he would say, "Death has come to my bedside; I have been through enough of work and play; let the world realize what contribution I have made; it will take quite a long time to understand that". (*ND* 4: 521)

14. In an October 13, 1898 letter to Mrs. Ashton Jonson, written from Kashmir, Sister Nivedita described Swami Vivekananda's spiritual mood:

To him at this moment "doing good" seems horrible. "Only the Mother does anything. Patriotism is a mistake. Everything is a mistake. It is all Mother. . . . All men are good. Only we cannot *reach* all. . . . I am never going to teach any more. Who am I that I should teach anyone? . . . Swamiji is dead and gone." (*ND* 5: 3-4)

15. From Mr. Sachindranath Basu's letter recounting Swami Vivekananda's closing remarks in his talk to swamis and novices assembled at Belur Math, June 19, 1899:

"My sons, all of you be men. This is what I want! If you are even a little successful, I shall feel my life has been meaningful." (*ND* 5: 17)

16. During an evening talk with Swami Saradananda in the spring of 1899:

"Men should be taught to be practical, physically strong. A dozen such lions will conquer the world, not millions of sheep. Men should not be taught to imitate a personal ideal, however great." (*ND* 5: 17)

17. From Mrs. Mary C. Funke's reminiscences of her August 1899 voyage to America with Swamis Vivekananda and Turiyananda:

"And if all this Maya is so beautiful, think of the wondrous beauty of the Reality behind it!" (*ND* 5: 76)

"Why recite poetry when there [pointing to sea and sky] is the very essence of poetry?" (Ibid.)

18. In Miss Josephine MacLeod's September 3, 1899 letter to Mrs. Ole Bull:

"In one's greatest hour of need one stands alone." (*ND* 5: 122)

19. From Sister Nivedita's October 27, 1899 diary entry at Ridgely Manor, in which Swami Vivekananda expressed his concern for Olea Bull Vaughn:

"Nightmares always begin pleasantly — only at the worst point [the] dream is broken — so death breaks [the] dream of life. Love death." (*ND* 5: 138)

20. In a December 1899 letter from Miss Josephine MacLeod to Sister Nivedita:

"All the ideas the Californians have of me emanated from Chicago." (*ND* 5: 179)

21. From Mrs. Alice Hansbrough's reminiscences which quoted Swami Vivekananda as telling Mr. Baumgardt:

"I can talk on the same subject, but it will not be the same lecture." (*ND* 5: 230)

22. Mrs. Alice Hansbrough's reminiscences relating Swami Vivekananda's response to her sight-seeing attempts:

"Do not show me sights. I have seen the Himalayas! I would not go ten steps to see sights; but I would go a thousand miles to see a [great] human being!" (*ND* 5: 244)

23. From Mrs. Alice Hansbrough's reminiscences relating Swami Vivekananda's interest in the problem of child training:

He did not believe in punishment. It had never helped him, he said, and added, "I would never do anything to make a child afraid". (*ND* 5: 253)

24. Mrs. Alice Hansbrough's record of Swami Vivekananda's explanation of God to seventeen-year-old Ralph Wyckoff:

"Can you see your own eyes? God is like that. He is as close as your own eyes. He is your own, even though you can't see Him." (*ND* 5: 254)

25. Mrs. Alice Hansbrough's reminiscences regarding Swami Vivekananda's opinion of the low-caste English soldiers who occupied India:

"If anyone should despoil the Englishman's home, the Englishman would kill him, and rightly so. But the Hindu just sits and whines!

"Do you think that a handful of Englishmen could rule India if we had a militant spirit? I teach meat-eating throughout the length and breadth of India in the hope that we can build a militant spirit!" (*ND* 5: 256)

26. Mrs. Alice Hansbrough's reminiscences of a picnic in Pasadena, California when a Christian Science woman suggested to Swami Vivekananda that one should teach people to be good:

"Why should I desire to be 'good'? All this is His handiwork [waving his hand to indicate the trees and the countryside]. Shall I apologize for His handiwork? If you want to reform John Doe, go and live with him; don't try to reform him. If you have any of the Divine Fire, he will catch it." (*ND* 5: 257)

27. From Mrs. Alice Hansbrough's reminiscences:

"When once you consider an action, do not let anything dissuade you. Consult your heart, not others, and then follow its dictates." (*ND* 5: 311)

28. From Mr. Frank Rhodehamel's notes taken during a March 1900 lecture in Oakland, California:

"Never loved a husband the wife for the wife's sake, or the wife the husband for the husband's sake. It is God in the wife the husband loves, and God in the husband the wife loves. (Cf. Brihadâranyaka Upanishad II.4.5.) It is God in everyone that draws us to that one in love. [It is] God in everything, in everybody that makes us love. God is the only love. . . . In everyone is God, the Atman; all else is but dream, an illusion." (*ND* 5: 362)

29. From Mr. Frank Rhodehamel's notes taken during a March 1900 lecture in Oakland, California:

Oh, if you only knew yourselves! You are souls; you are gods. If ever I feel [that I am] blaspheming, it is when I call you man." (*ND* 5: 362)

30. An excerpt from Mr. Thomas J. Allan's reminiscences of Swami Vivekananda's March 1900 San Francisco lecture series on India:

"Send us mechanics to teach us how to use our hands, and we will send you missionaries to teach you spirituality." (*ND* 5: 365)

31. Mrs. Edith Allan's reminiscences of Swami Vivekananda's philosophical observations while cooking at the Turk Street flat:

"'The Lord dwells in the hearts of all beings, O Arjuna, by His illusive power causing all beings to revolve as though mounted on a potter's wheel.' [Bhagavad-Gitâ XVIII.61] This has all happened before, like the throw of a dice, so it is in life; the wheel goes on and the same combination comes up; that pitcher and glass have stood there before, so, too, that onion and potato. What can we do, Madam, He has us on the wheel of life." (ND 6: 17)

32. From Mrs. Edith Allan's reminiscences of an after-lunch conversation:

"The Master said he would come again in about two hundred years — and I will come with him. When a Master comes, he brings his own people." (ND 6: 17)

33. Mrs. Edith Allan's reminiscences of Swami Vivekananda's "kitchen" counsel while he was staying in San Francisco, California, in 1900:

"If I consider myself greater than the ant that crawls on the ground I am ignorant." (ND 6: 19)

"Madam, be broad—minded; always see two ways. When I am on the heights I say, 'Shivoham, Shivoham: I am He, I am He!' and when I have the stomachache I say, 'Mother have mercy on me!'" (Ibid.)

"Learn to be the witness. If two dogs are fighting on the street and I go out there, I get mixed up in the fight; but if I stay quietly in my room, I witness the fight from the window. So learn to be the witness." (Ibid.)

34. From Mr. Thomas J. Allan's reminiscences of a private talk with Swami Vivekananda in San Francisco, California, 1900:

"We do not progress from error to truth, but from truth to truth. Thus we must see that none can be blamed for what they are doing, because they are, at this time, doing the best they can. If a child has an open razor, don't try to take it from him, but give him a red apple or a brilliant toy, and he will drop the razor. But he who puts his hand in the fire will be burned; we learn only from experience." (ND 6: 42)

35. From Mrs. Alice Hansbrough's reminiscences of a walk home with Swami Vivekananda after one of his lectures in San Francisco in 1900:

"You have heard that Christ said, 'My words are spirit and they are life'. So are my words spirit and life; they will burn their way into your brain and you will never get away from them!" (ND 6: 57-58)

36. From Mrs. Alice Hansbrough's reminiscences in San Francisco, 1900 — referring to Swami Vivekananda's great heart:

"I may have to be born again because I have fallen in love with man." (ND 6: 79)

37. From Mrs. George Roorbach's reminiscences of Swami Vivekananda at Camp Taylor, California, in May 1900:

"In my first speech in this country, in Chicago, I addressed that audience as 'Sisters and Brothers of America', and you know that they all rose to their feet. You may wonder what made them do this, you may wonder if I had some strange power. Let me tell you that I did have a power and this is it — never once in my life did I allow myself to have even one sexual thought. I trained my mind, my thinking, and the powers that man usually uses along that line I put into a higher channel, and it developed a force so strong that nothing could resist it." (*ND* 6: 155)

38. In a conversation with Swami Turiyananda, which probably took place in New York:

"The call has come from Above: 'Come away, just come away — no need of troubling your head to teach others'. It is now the will of the Grand Old Lady (The "Grand Old Lady" was a figure in a children's game, whose touch put one outside the game.) that the play should be over." (*ND* 6: 373)

39. In a July 1902 Prabuddha Bharata eulogy, "a Western disciple" wrote:

The Swami had but scant sympathy with iconoclasts, for as he wisely remarked, "The true philosopher strives to destroy nothing, but to help all". (*VIN*: 638)

40. Sister Nivedita's reminiscences of Swami Vivekananda in an October 9, 1899 letter to Miss Josephine MacLeod:

He has turned back on so much — "Let your life in the world be nothing but a thinking to yourself". (*LSN* I: 213)

41. Swami Vivekananda's luncheon remarks to Mrs. Ole Bull, recorded by Sister Nivedita in an October 18, 1899 letter to Miss Josephine MacLeod:

"You see, there is one thing called love, and there is another thing called union. And union is greater than love.

"I do not love religion. I have become identified with it. It is my life. So no man loves that thing in which his life has been spent, in which he really has accomplished something. That which we love is not yet ourself. Your husband did not love music for which he had always stood. He loved engineering in which as yet he knew comparatively little. This is the difference between Bhakti and Jnana; and this is why Jnana is greater than Bhakti." (*LSN* I: 216)

42. Swami Vivekananda's remarks on his spiritual ministry, recorded in Sister Nivedita's October 15, 1904 letter to Miss Josephine MacLeod:

"Only when they go away will they know how much they have received." (*LSN* II: 686)

43. Sister Nivedita's reminiscences in a November 5, 1904 letter to Alberta Sturges (Lady Sandwich) of Swami Vivekananda's talk on renunciation while he was staying at Ridgely Manor:

"In India we never say that you should renounce a higher thing for a lower. It is better to be absorbed in music or in literature than in comfort or pleasure, and we never say otherwise." (*LSN* II: 690)

44. In Sister Nivedita's November 19, 1909 letter to Miss Josephine MacLeod:

"The fire burns if we plunge our hand in — whether we feel it or not — so it is with him who speaks the name of God." (*LSN* II: 1030)

45. Swami Vivekananda's reminiscences of Shri Ramakrishna, recorded in Sister Nivedita's July 6, 1910 letter to Dr. T. K. Cheyne:

"He could not imagine himself the teacher of anyone. He was like a man playing with balls of many colours, and leaving it to others to select which they would for themselves." (*LSN* II: 1110)

46. Sister Nivedita's reminiscences of a conversation with Swami Vivekananda at Ridgely Manor, recorded in an 1899 letter written from Ridgely Manor to Miss Josephine MacLeod:

I have never heard the Prophet talk so much of Shri Ramakrishna. He told us what I had heard before of [his master's] infallible judgement of men. . . .

"And so", Swami said, "you see my devotion is the dog's devotion. I have been wrong so often and he has always been right, and now I trust his judgement blindly". And then he told us how he would hypnotize anyone who came to him and in two minutes know all about him, and Swami said that from this he had learnt to count our consciousness as a very small thing. (*LSN* II: 1263)

47. From Sister Nivedita's January 27, 1900 letter to Sister Christine:

Swami said today that he is beginning to see the needs of humanity in quite a different light — that he is already sure of the principle that is to help, but is spending hours every day in trying to solve the methods. That what he had known hitherto is for men living in a cave — alone, undisturbed — but now he will give "humanity something that will make for strength in the stress of daily life". (*LSN* II: 1264)

48. In a July 7, 1902 letter to Sister Christine, Sister Nivedita recorded one of Swami Vivekananda's remarks made while giving a class to the monks at Belur Math on July 4, 1902:

"Do not copy me. Kick out the man who imitates." (LSN II: 1270)

49. The Swami's comment after he made a statement concerning the ideal of the freedom of the soul, which brought it into apparent conflict with the Western conception of the service of humanity as the goal of the individual:

"You will say that this does not benefit society. But before this objection can be admitted you will first have to prove that the maintenance of society is an object in itself." (CWSN 1: 19)

50. Sister Nivedita wrote:

He touched on the question of his own position as a wandering teacher and expressed the Indian diffidence with regard to religious organization or, as someone expresses it, "with regard to a faith that ends in a church". "We believe", he said, "that organization always breeds new evils".

He prophesied that certain religious developments then much in vogue in the West would speedily die, owing to love of money. And he declared that "Man proceeds from truth to truth, and not from error to truth". (CWSN 1: 19-20)

51. "The universe is like a cobweb and minds are the spiders; for mind is one as well as many." (*CWSN* 1: 21)

52. "Let none regret that they were difficult to convince! I fought my Master for six years with the result that I know every inch of the way! Every inch of the way!" (*CWSN* 1: 22)

53. Swami Vivekananda was elucidating to what heights of selflessness the path of love leads and how it draws out the very best faculties of the soul:

"Suppose there were a baby in the path of the tiger! Where would your place be then? At his mouth — any one of you — I am sure of it." (CWSN 1: 24)

54. "That by which all this is pervaded, know *That* to be the Lord Himself!" (*CWSN* 1: 27)

55. Concerning Swami Vivekananda's attitude toward religion:

Religion was a matter of the growth of the individual, "a question always of being and becoming". (CWSN 1: 28)

56. "Forgive when you also can bring legions of angels to an easy victory." While victory was still doubtful, however, only a coward to his thinking would turn the other cheek. (*CWSN* 1: 28-29)

57. "Of course I would commit a crime and go to hell forever if by that I could really help a human being!" (*CWSN* 1: 34)

58. To a small group, including Sister Nivedita, after a lecture:

"I have a superstition — it is nothing, you know, but a personal superstition! — that the same soul who came once as Buddha came afterwards as Christ." (*CWSN* 1: 35)

59. After Swami Vivekananda was told of Sister Nivedita's willingness to serve India:

"For my own part I will be incarnated two hundred times, if that is necessary, to do this work amongst my people that I have undertaken." (*CWSN* 1: 36)

60. Sister Nivedita's memory of an incident:

He was riding on one occasion with the Raja of Khetri, when he saw that his arm was bleeding profusely and found that the wound had been caused by a thorny branch which he had held aside for himself to pass. When the Swami expostulated, the Rajput laughed the matter aside. "Are we not always the defenders of the faith, Swamiji?" he said.

"And then", said the Swami, telling the story, "I was just going to tell him that they ought not to show such honour to the Sannyasin, when suddenly I thought that perhaps they were right after all. Who knows? Maybe I too am caught in the glare of this flashlight of your modern civilization, which is only for a moment".

" — I have become entangled", he said simply to one who protested that to his mind the wandering Sâdhu of earlier years, who had scattered his knowledge and changed his name as he went, had been greater than the abbot of Belur, burdened with much work and many cares. "I have become entangled." (*CWSN* 1: 43)

61. Sister Nivedita wrote:

One day he was talking in the West of Mirâ Bâi — that saint who once upon a time was Queen of Chitore — and of the freedom her husband had offered her if only she would remain within the royal seclusion. But she could not be bound. "But why should she not?" someone asked in astonishment. "Why should she?" he retorted. "Was she living down here in this mire?" (*CWSN* 1: 44)

62. As years went by, the Swami dared less and less to make determinate plans or dogmatize about the unknown:

"After all, what do we know? Mother uses it all. But we are only fumbling about." (*CWSN* 1: 44)

63. Quoting Swami Vivekananda, Sister Nivedita remembered:

Love was not love, it was insisted, unless it was "without a reason" or without a "motive" . . . . (*CWSN* 1: 52)

64. About Swami Vivekananda, Sister Nivedita wrote:

When asked by some of his own people what he considered, after seeing them in their own country, to be the greatest achievement of the English, he answered "that they had known how to combine obedience with self-respect". (*CWSN* 1: 54)

65. Swami Sadananda reported that early in the morning, while it was still dark, Swami Vivekananda would rise and call the others, singing:

"Awake! Awake! all ye who would drink of the divine nectar!" (CWSN 1: 56)

66. Sister Nivedita remembered:

At this time [during the Swami's itinerant days, near Almora] he passed some months in a cave overhanging a mountain village. Only twice have I known him to allude to this experience. Once he said, "Nothing in my whole life ever so filled me with the sense of work to be done. It was as if I were thrown out from that life in caves to wander to and fro in the plains below". And again he said to someone, "It is not the form of his life that makes a Sadhu. For it is possible to sit in a cave and have one's whole mind filled with the question of how many pieces of bread will be brought to one for supper!" (*CWSN* 1: 61)

67. About his own poem "Kali the Mother":

"Scattering plagues and sorrows", he quoted from his own verses,

> *Dancing mad with joy,*
> *Come, Mother, come!*
> *For terror is Thy name!*
> *Death — is in Thy breath.*
> *And every shaking step*
> *Destroys a world for e'er.*

"It all came true, every word of it", he interrupted himself to say.

> *Who dares misery love.*
> *Dance in Destruction's dance,*
> *And hug the form of death, . . .*

"To him the Mother does indeed come. I have proved it. For I have hugged the form of Death!" (CWSN 1: 98-99)

68. Sister Nivedita, referring to her plans for a girls' school:

Only in one respect was he [Swami Vivekananda] inflexible. The work for the education of Indian women, to which he would give his name, might be as sectarian as I chose to make it. "You wish through a sect to rise beyond all sects." (CWSN 1: 102)

69. Commenting on Sister Nivedita's visit to Gopaler-Ma's dwelling — a small cell:

"Ah! this is the old India that you have seen, the India of prayers and tears, of vigils and fasts, that is passing away, never to return!" (CWSN 1: 109)

70. About the aims of the Ramakrishna Order:

The same purpose spoke again in his definition of the aims of the Order of Ramakrishna — "to effect an exchange of the highest ideals of the East and the West and to realize these in practice" . . . . (CWSN 1: 113)

71. After teaching Sister Nivedita the worship of Shiva, Swami Vivekananda then culminated it in an offering of flowers at the feet of the Buddha. He said, as if addressing each soul that would ever come to him for guidance:

"Go thou and follow Him, who was born and gave His life for others five hundred times before He attained the vision of the Buddha!" (CWSN 1: 114)

72. Upon returning from a pilgrimage in Kashmir:

"These gods are not merely symbols! They are the forms that the Bhaktas have seen!" (CWSN 1: 120)

73. Sister Nivedita's reminiscences of Swami Vivekananda's words heard long before:

"The Impersonal God seen through the mists of sense is personal." (CWSN 1: 120)

74. Swami Vivekananda's comment when he was reminded of the rareness of criminality in India:

"Would God it were otherwise in my land, for this is verily the virtuousness of death!" (CWSN 1: 123)

75. Swami Vivekananda said:

"The whole of life is only a swan song! Never forget those lines:

> *The lion, when stricken to the heart,*
> *gives out his mightiest roar.*
> *When smitten on the head, the cobra lifts its hood.*
> *And the majesty of the soul comes forth,*
> *only when a man is wounded to his depths."*

(CWSN 1: 124)

76. After hearing of the death of Shri Durga Charan Nag (Nag Mahashay):

"[He] was one of the greatest of the works of Ramakrishna Paramahamsa." (CWSN 1: 129)

77. About Shri Ramakrishna's transformative power, Swami Vivekananda said:

"Was it a joke that Ramakrishna Paramahamsa should touch a life? Of course he made new men and new women of those who came to him, even in these fleeting contacts!" (CWSN 1: 130)

78. While speaking on the true spirit of a Sannyasin, Swami Vivekananda said:

"I saw many great men in Hrishikesh. One case that I remember was that of a man who seemed to be mad. He was coming nude down the street, with boys pursuing and throwing stones at him. The whole man was bubbling over with laughter while blood was streaming down his face and neck. I took him and bathed the wound, putting ashes on it to stop the bleeding. And all the time with peals of laughter he told me of the fun the boys and he had been having, throwing the stones. 'So the Father plays', he said.

"Many of these men hide, in order to guard themselves against intrusion. People are a trouble to them. One had human bones strewn about his cave and gave it out that he lived on corpses. Another threw stones. And so on. . . .

"Sometimes the thing comes upon them in a flash. There was a boy, for instance, who used to come to read the Upanishads with Abhedananda. One day he turned and said, 'Sir, is all this really true?'

"'Oh yes!' said Abhedananda, 'It may be difficult to realize, but it is certainly true'.

"And next day, that boy was a silent Sannyasin, nude, on his way to Kedarnath!

"What happened to him? you ask. He became silent!

"But the Sannyasin needs no longer to worship or to go on pilgrimage or perform austerities. What then is the motive of all this going from pilgrimage to pilgrimage, shrine to shrine, and austerity to austerity? He is acquiring merit and giving it to the world!" (CWSN 1: 133)

79. Referring to the story of Shibi Rana:

"Ah yes! These are the stories that are deep in our nation's heart! Never forget that the Sannyasin takes two vows: one to realize the truth and one to help the world — and that the most stringent of stringent requirements is that he should renounce any thought of heaven!" (CWSN 1: 134)

80. To Sister Nivedita:

"The Gitâ says that there are three kinds of charity: the Tâmasic, the Râjasic and the Sâttvic. Tamasic charity is performed on an impulse. It is always making mistakes. The doer thinks of nothing but his own impulse to be kind. Rajasic charity is what a man does for his own glory. And Sattvic charity is that which is given to the right person, in the right way, and at the proper time. . . .

"When it comes to the Sattvic, I think more and more of a certain great Western woman in whom I have seen that quiet giving, always to the right person in the right way, at the right time, and never making a mistake.

"For my own part, I have been learning that even charity can go too far. . . .

"As I grow older I find that I look more and more for greatness in little things. I want to know what a great man eats and wears, and how he speaks to his servants. I want to find a Sir Philip Sidney (Sir Philip Sidney (1554-1586): English poet, soldier and politician.) greatness! Few men would remember the thirst of others, even in the moment of death.

"But anyone will be great in a great position! Even the coward will grow brave in the glare of the footlights. The world looks on. Whose heart will not throb? Whose pulse will not quicken till he can do his best?

"More and more the true greatness seems to me that of the worm doing its duty silently, steadily, from moment to moment and from hour to hour." (*CWSN* 1: 137)

81. Referring to the great individual — the divine incarnation, the Guru, and the Rishi:

"You do not yet understand India! We Indians are man — worshippers, after all! Our God is man!" (*CWSN* 1: 144)

82. On another occasion, Swami Vivekananda used the word "man-worshippers" in an entirely different sense:

"This idea of man—worship exists in nucleus in India, but it has never been expanded. You must develop it. Make poetry, make art, of it. Establish the worship of the feet of beggars as you had it in Mediaeval Europe. Make man-worshippers." (*CWSN* 1: 144-45)

83. To Sister Nivedita:

"There is a peculiar sect of Mohammedans who are reported to be so fanatical that they take each newborn babe and expose it, saying, 'If God made thee, perish! If Ali made thee, live!' Now this, which they say to the child, I say, but in the opposite sense, to you tonight: 'Go forth into the world and there, if I made you, be destroyed! If Mother made you, live'!" (*CWSN* 1: 151)

84. Long after Southern magnates in America had apologized to Vivekananda when they learned that he had been mistaken for a Negro and was thus refused admission into hotels, the Swami remarked to himself:

"What! rise at the expense of another! I didn't come to earth for that! . . . If I am grateful to my white-skinned Aryan ancestor, I am far more so to my yellow-skinned Mongolian ancestor and, most so of all, to the black-skinned Negritoid!" (*CWSN* 1: 153)

85. Commenting on the dungeon-cages of mediaeval prisoners on Mont-Saint-Michel:

"What a wonderful place for meditation!" (*CWSN* 1: 154)

"Oh, I know I have wandered over the whole earth, but in India I have looked for nothing save the cave in which to meditate!" (Ibid.)

86. Though he considered offspring of the Roman Empire to be brutal and the Japanese notion of marriage a horror, Swami Vivekananda nevertheless summed up the constructive ideals, never the defects, of a community:

"For patriotism, the Japanese! For purity, the Hindu! And for manliness, the European! There is no other in the world who understands, as does the Englishman, what should be the glory of a man!" (CWSN 1: 160)

87. Swami Vivekananda said of himself before he left for America in 1893:

"I go forth to preach a religion of which Buddhism is nothing but a rebel child and Christianity, with all her pretensions, only a distant echo!" (CWSN 1: 161)

88. Describing the night Buddha left his wife to renounce the world, Swami Vivekananda said:

"What was the problem that vexed him? Why! It was she whom he was about to sacrifice for the world! That was the struggle! He cared nothing for himself!" (CWSN 1: 172)

89. After describing Buddha's touching farewell to his wife, the Swami said:

"Have you never thought of the hearts of the heroes? How they were great, great, great — and soft as butter?" (CWSN 1: 172)

90. Swami Vivekananda's description of Buddha's death and its similarity with that of Shri Ramakrishna's:

He told how the blanket had been spread for him beneath the tree and how the Blessed One had lain down, "resting on his right side like a lion" to die, when suddenly there came to him one who ran for instruction. The disciples would have treated the man as an intruder, maintaining peace at any cost about their Master's death-bed, but the Blessed One overheard, and saying, "No, no! He who was sent (Lit., "the Tathâgata". "A word", explained Swami Vivekananda, "which is very like your 'Messiah'".) is ever ready", he raised himself on his elbow and taught. This happened four times and then, and then only, Buddha held himself free to die. "But first he spoke to reprove Ananda for weeping. The Buddha was not a person but a realization, and to that any one of them might attain. And with his last breath he forbade them to worship any."

*The immortal story went on to its end. But to one who listened, the most significant moment had been that in which the teller paused — at his own words "raised himself on his elbow and taught" — and said, in brief parenthesis, "*I saw this, you know, in the case of Ramakrishna Paramahamsa". And there rose before the mind the story of one, destined to learn from that teacher, who had travelled a hundred miles, and arrived at Cossipore only when he lay dying. Here also the disciples would have refused admission, but Shri Ramakrishna intervened, insisting on receiving the new-comer, and teaching him. (*CWSN* 1: 175-176)

91. *Commenting on the historic and philosophic significance of Buddhistic doctrine:*

"Form, feeling, sensation, motion and knowledge are the five categories in perpetual flux and fusion. And in these lies Maya. Of any one wave nothing can be predicated, for it is not. It but was and is gone. Know, O Man, thou art the sea! Ah, this was Kapila's philosophy, but his great disciple [Buddha] brought the heart to make it live!" (*CWSN* 1: 176)

92. *Concerning the Buddhist First Council and the dispute as to its President:*

"Can you imagine what their strength was? One said it should be Ananda, because he had loved Him most. But someone else stepped forward and said no! for Ananda had been guilty of weeping at the death-bed. And so he was passed over!" (*CWSN* 1: 177)

93. *Considering reincarnation a "scientific speculation" rather than an article of faith:*

"Why, one life in the body is like a million years of confinement, and they want to wake up the memory of many lives! Sufficient unto the day is the evil thereof! . . . Yes! Buddhism must be right! Reincarnation is only a mirage! But this vision is to be reached by the path of Advaita alone!" (*CWSN* 1: 180-81)

94. "Had I lived in Palestine, in the days of Jesus of Nazareth, I would have washed his feet, not with my tears, but with my heart's blood!" (*CWSN* 1: 189)

95. *"For the Advaitin, therefore, the only* motive is love. . . . It is the Saviour who should go on his way rejoicing, not the saved!" (*CWSN* 1: 197-98)

96. *On the necessity of restraint in a disciple's life:*

"Struggle to realize yourself without a trace of emotion! . . . Watch the fall of the leaves, but gather the sentiment of the sight from within at some later time!" (CWSN 1: 207)

"Mind! No loaves and fishes! No glamour of the world! All this must be cut short. It must be rooted out. It is sentimentality—the overflow of the senses. It comes to you in colour, sight, sound, and associations. Cut it off. Learn to hate it. It is utter poison!" (Ibid., 207-208)

97. *On the value of types:*

"Two diffferent races mix and fuse, and out of them rises one strong distinct type. A strong and distinct type is always the physical basis of the horizon. It is all

very well to talk of universalism, but the world will not be ready for that for millions of years!

"Remember! if you want to know what a ship is like, the ship has to be specified as it is — its length, breadth, shape, and material. And to understand a nation, we must do the same. India is idolatrous. You must help her *as she is*. Those who have left her can do nothing for her!" (CWSN 1: 209)

98. Describing the Indian ideal of Brahmacharya in the student's life, Swami Vivekananda said:

"Brahmacharya should be like a burning fire within the veins!" (CWSN 1: 216)

99. Concerning marriage by arrangement instead of choice, Swami Vivekananda said:

"There is such pain in this country! Such pain! Some, of course, there must always have been. But now the sight of Europeans with their different customs has increased it. Society knows that there is another way!

[To a European] "We have exalted motherhood and you, wifehood: and I think both might gain by some interchange.

"In India the wife must not dream of loving even a son as she loves her husband. She must be Sati. But the husband ought not to love his wife as he does his mother. Hence a reciprocated affection is not thought so high as one unreturned. It is 'shopkeeping'. The joy of the contact of husband and wife is not admitted in India. This we have to borrow from the West. Our ideal needs to be refreshed by yours. And you, in turn, need something of our devotion to motherhood." (CWSN 1: 221-22)

100. Speaking to a disciple with great compassion:

"You need not mind if these shadows of home and marriage cross your mind sometimes. Even to me, they come now and again!" (CWSN 1: 222)

101. On hearing of the intense loneliness of a friend:

"Every worker feels like that at times!" (CWSN 1: 222)

102. Concerning the Hindu and Buddhist monastic and non-monastic ideals:

"The glory of Hinduism lies in the fact that while it has defined ideals, it has never dared to say that any one of these alone was the one true way. In this it differs from Buddhism, which exalts monasticism above all others as the path that must be taken by all souls to reach perfection. The story given in the Mahâbhârata of the young saint who was made to seek enlightenment, first from a married woman and then from a butcher, is sufficient to show this. 'By doing my duty', said each one of these when asked, 'by doing my duty in my own station, have I attained

this knowledge'. There is no career then which might not be the path to God. The question of attainment depends only, in the last resort, on the thirst of the soul." (*CWSN* 1: 223)

103. With reference to the idea that the lover always sees the ideal in the beloved, Swami Vivekananda responded to a girl's newly avowed love:

"Cling to this vision! As long as you can both see the ideal in one another, your worship and happiness will grow more instead of less." (*CWSN* 1: 224)

104. "The highest truth is always the simplest." (CWSN 1: 226)

105. Swami Vivekananda's remarks on American séances:

"Always the greatest fraud by the simplest means." (*CWSN* 1: 233)

106. On Western and Eastern views of a person as a body or a soul:

"Western languages declare that man is a body and has a soul; Eastern languages declare that he is a soul and has a body." (*CWSN* 1: 236-37)

107. Concerning Swami Vivekananda's reverence for his Guru:

"I can criticize even an Avatâra [divine incarnation] without the slightest diminution of my love for him! But I know quite well that most people are not so; and for them it is safest to protect their own Bhakti!" (CWSN 1: 252)

"Mine is the devotion of the dog! I don't want to know why! I am contented simply to follow!" (Ibid., 252-53)

108. "Ramakrishna Paramahamsa used to begin every day by walking about in his room for a couple of hours, saying 'Satchidânanda!' or 'Shivoham!' or some other holy word." (CWSN 1: 255)

109. A few months before his passing away, Swami Vivekananda said:

"How often does a man ruin his disciples by remaining always with them! When men are once trained, it is essential that their leader leaves them; for without his absence they cannot develop themselves!" (*CWSN* 1: 260)

110. A few days before his passing away, the Swami said:

"I am making ready for death. A great Tapasyâ and meditation has come upon me, and I am making ready for death." (CWSN 1: 261-62)

111. In Kashmir after an illness, Swami Vivekananda said as he lifted a couple of pebbles:

"Whenever death approaches me, all weakness vanishes. I have neither fear, nor doubt, nor thought of the external. I simply busy myself making ready to die. I am as hard as that [the pebbles struck one another in his hand] — for I *have* touched the feet of God!" (*CWSN* 1: 262)